the
Complete
DOVETAIL

the *Complete* DOVETAIL

HANDMADE FURNITURE'S SIGNATURE JOINT

Ian Kirby

LINDEN PUBLISHING
Fresno, CA

The Complete Dovetail

By

Ian Kirby
Originally published by the Cambium Press 1999
First Linden Publishing edition 2001
ISBN-13: 978-0-941936-67-5
ISBN-10: 0-941936-67-8
© Ian Kirby 1999

Library of Congress Cataloging-in-Publication Data

Kirby, Ian J., 1932-
   The complete dovetail :handmade furniture's signature joint / by Ian Kirby.--1st Linden
Publishing ed.
      p. Cm
   Originally published: Newton, CT : Cambium,1999
   Includes index.
   ISBN 0-941936-67-8 (pbk.)
   1. Furniture making. 2. Timber joints. I. Title

TT194.K57 2001
683.1'04--dc21   2001029575

The Woodworkers Library™

Linden Publishing, Inc.
2006 South Mary
Fresno, CA 93721
800-345-4447
www.lindenpub.com

Printed in the United States of America

CONTENTS

Dovetails – simple, solid, elegant

Because every woodworker comes to the subject of dovetail joinery with unique skills, tools, and aspirations, it follows that each woodworker will find this handbook useful in a different way. Some readers may be skilled in the use of all the tools, but may never have cut a dovetail joint. Others may be using one, some, or all of the tools for the first time. You may wish to specialize in one particular type of dovetail, say, a single lap commonly used for drawers while another reader may wish to become a skilled maker of all four major types.

Whatever the circumstances, I have to dispel a widely held notion about the complexity of the joint and the difficulty of making it. No special tool skills are required. Marking, sawing, and paring skills are everyday woodworking requirements not limited to making dovetails.

Consider the through dovetail for example. All you are doing is sawing down a line for about 3/4 in. (19 mm) in wood that's about 3/4-in. thick. That's like cutting a piece of wood 3/4-in. square in two – so how difficult can that be? You then have to remove the waste wood in one way or another and finish by squaring the shoulders.

What is specific to making dovetails by hand, however, is the methodology. Unless you understand the order of work, dovetails will remain complex and impossible to make accurately.

This book explains the making of the joint in its various forms. It doesn't attempt to connect all the links in the chain of events before and after the joint is used in a piece of furniture. I begin by demonstrating marking, sawing and chiseling skills. Next, the skills are practiced as separate exercises, then the order of work is explained, and, finally, you make complete joints.

A Craft Heritage

I'm a self-taught woodworker.

You have heard this statement so many times that you may believe that there's no other way to learn to woodwork. How discouraging it must be to feel that you are on your own without any well-formulated body of knowledge to guide you. Fortunately, it's not true. I am not self-taught. I had great teachers, lots of them, so it saddens me that so many people who are interested in this craft feel they have to "go it alone."

Our techniques of working solid wood are no accident. From the 1400s they were passed on by word of mouth and by example, from master to apprentice, right there in the workshop. The high point occurred a hundred years ago, a time of great activity in a wide range of crafts.

It was called the Arts and Crafts Movement, and it had far-reaching effects in Europe and the United States. Today its key figures and practitioners are long gone and its products museum pieces, but the tenets that guided the movement are still important to those of us who care about woodworking at the highest level.

Those tenets may be expressed as follows:

- the work should be designed in the simplest way
- it should be made of the best materials
- it should be constructed in a rightful manner

Rightful manner

Historians and archivists have written extensively about the first two tenets. I will expand on the third because it's germane to this book. Little has been written about constructing in a rightful manner because understanding what to do and how to do it cannot be gained from observation alone. No amount of time devoted to studying a completed through dovetail or a piece of furniture will reveal the skills required to make it or the working methods that determine in what order the work must be done.

This book focuses on the skills and methods of making dovetails in the rightful manner practiced by Arts and Crafts furniture makers. The determination of rightful manner is still relevant today and goes like this. There are a number of ways to get the job done. Take them all into account – analyze them, understand them, practice them – and before long one method will stand out because it produces the best results, measured by speed and efficiency, with no sacrifice of quality. Adopt this method as the rightful manner while remaining open to further improvements.

The outcome of this rigorous procedure were tool skills, working methods, and a common vocabulary that formed the heart of of a professional workshop of the time. Today, professional woodworking has changed so radically that except in rare places inhabited by rare people, the skills and methods which marked the zenith of this form of professional woodworking practice only a few decades ago have disappeared from the shop floor.

Continuing the tradition

Does this mean that the old methods are redundant? Not at all. Practically all of them hold good today – and why wouldn't they? They were fashioned, refined, and practiced by thoughtful, highly skilled, professional woodworkers. Their importance remains unchanged, only the practitioner differs. Established in a small workshop, with tools still affordable and methods still vital, the amateur woodworker and small-shop professional can produce furniture to rival the best ever made by anyone.

My own experience was with men who were the direct recipients of the Arts and Crafts movement – Edward Barnsley, Reggie Gough, Mo Okenden, Cramper Lewis, Eric Drake, Ken Bowers, to name a few. It was a time when what is contained in this book was common knowledge. Unfortunately, the makers of that time concentrated their energy solely on designing and making furniture. Had they produced books as well, their writings would comprise the standard works of reference that we so sorely lack. This book gives you a small piece of the story. It's up to you to embrace the practice and spread the word.

CHAPTER 1

The dovetail family

The antiquity of woodworking joints is impossible to determine because wood, compared to other worked materials like stone and pottery, is perishable. However, the dry climate of Egypt has been relatively kind to wood and from that region we get an inkling of the long ancestry of joint design and making in the form of wooden coffins from the Old Kingdom. Made some 3,500 years ago, they contain several types of joint, including dovetails.

So as you take up saw, chisel, and mallet you are continuing a very long tradition with tools that have changed very little over the ages. However, the joint has grown in versatility and sophistication. It can be a corner joint with its structure visible or hidden, it can join wide boards at right angles other than at the corners, and it can be a rail joint.

Four members of the dovetail family are used to join wide boards at their ends to form corners. They are:

- through dovetail
- single lap dovetail
- double lap dovetail
- secret miter dovetail

These four are principal members of the family. Other relatives include the dovetail halving, the dovetail housing, and the drawer top rail. See Chapter 8 for how to make and use these joints.

The four principal joints are listed in order of complexity. As you progress from one to the other, you will learn something new, but you will also carry forward everything you learned in making the previous joint.

Amateur and small professional shops use a mix of hand and machine tools for reasons of preference, economy, and versatility. The pleasures of handwork are many: noise is negligible, dust is minimal, and the pace is human scale – all desirable benefits in a noisy, dusty, frenetic age.

Through dovetail

The through dovetail today symbolizes good workmanship. Being totally exposed, it announces clarity of purpose and honesty of structure.

Considered properly as an element of furniture design, the through dovetail is a "design detail." Barely visible from across the room, it comes into focus at a distance of 10 to 12 feet. That's when the observer begins to see the pattern of tails and pins and begins to appreciate the maker's intent. A closer look reveals how well the joint fits. However, no amount of inspection will reveal how it was made. If made in the simplest way, the two parts fit tight straight from the dovetail saw, with no chiseling of the sawn faces required.

I have included the cutting sequence of each joint at the outset to underscore how straightforward it is. If you already make the joint, compare my sequence to yours to see if any improvement is possible. If you've had limited success, consider what adaptations might be useful. And if you've never cut a dovetail, recognize that there is no mystery or magic in making a sequence of cuts.

Cutting sequence · Cut the slope of the tails with a dovetail saw. Remove the bulk of the waste with a coping saw. Make the bottom of the joint flat with a chisel. Using the tails as a template, mark the pins with a knife. Cut the pins with a dovetail saw. Remove the bulk of the waste with a coping saw. Make the bottom of the socket flat with a chisel. How to make a through dovetail is explained in Chapter 4.

Repeat performance Making the tails and pins of the through joint use essentially the same set of sawing and chiseling techniques.

The structural honesty of the through dovetail in solid wood furniture is often augmented by through-wedged mortise and tenon joints.

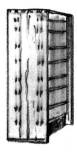

◄ *Bureau with through dovetail joint at top corners, hidden single lap dovetail on bottom corners, and through-wedged mortise and tenon joints for drawer rails.*

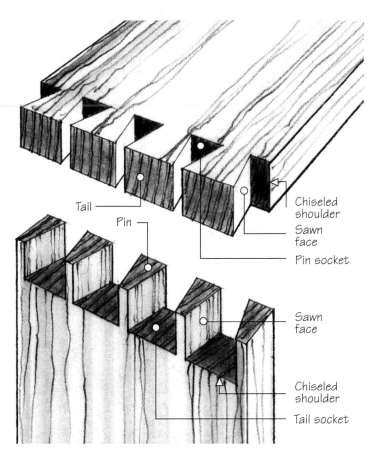

Tail

Pin

Chiseled shoulder

Sawn face

Pin socket

Sawn face

Chiseled shoulder

Tail socket

◀ **Principal parts** of a through dovetail, with square shoulders.

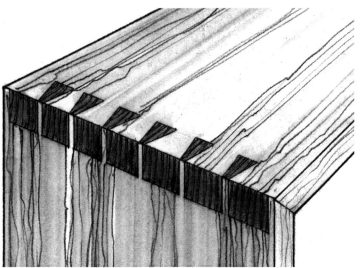

◀ **Through dovetail**, with mitered corner.

Single lap dovetail

Because drawers are a common element of furniture and because the single lap dovetail holds the fronts of drawers to the sides, it's the most used of the four corner joints.

The single lap dovetail is also used elsewhere on furniture, but in places where it cannot be seen. Imagine a sideboard with through dovetails on the top and bottom corners. The whole joint – pins and tails – is visible on the top, but only half the joint – the end grain of the tails – is visible on the bottom. To avoid this discordant, unbalanced, disconnected appearance, use a single lap on the bottom corner.

Cutting a single lap dovetail is more complex than cutting a through dovetail because you must chisel a closed socket, but the starting point is the same: cut the tails first.

Cutting sequence   Cut the slope of the tails with a dovetail saw. Remove the bulk of the waste with a coping saw. Make the bottom of the socket flat with a chisel. Using the tails as a template, mark the pins with a knife. Because of the lap on the pin piece, only a portion of the joint can be cut with a dovetail saw. Remove the bulk of the waste with a chisel and mallet. Finish the joint surfaces with skew and bench chisels. How to make a single lap dovetail is explained in Chapter 5.

Repeat performance   Making the tails for a single lap dovetail is the same as making the tails for a through joint. Making the pins requires a new technique.

The Arts and Crafts method of making a hand-made drawer, developed at the end of the 19th Century, represents a pinnacle of woodworking. There are more steps to its manufacture than any other structure in furniture making.

◄ *Single lap dovetails* are used at the bottom corners of this sideboard to avoid a visual conflict with the through dovetail on the top corners.

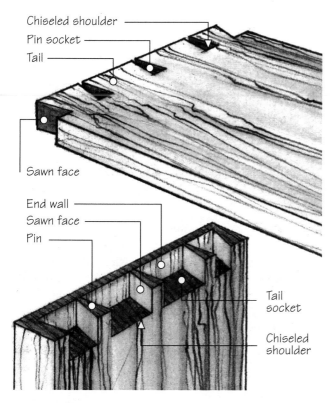

Chiseled shoulder

Pin socket

Tail

Sawn face

◀ *Principal parts* of *a single lap dovetail.*

End wall

Sawn face

Pin

Tail socket

Chiseled shoulder

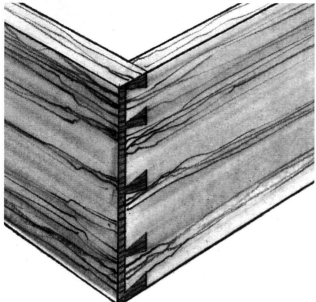

◀ *Single lap* dovetail *closed.*

Double lap dovetail

Unlike the previous two joints, the double lap dovetail and the secret miter dovetail are both invisible. When they're assembled, you can't see the pins and tails concealed inside. To visualize the construction of a double lap dovetail, think of a single lap joint; now put a pad of wood on the tail piece so that it's flush on all edges.

Of the two invisible dovetail joints, the double lap is the easier to make but the least used. Start by cutting the tails first – the same as as you would for the through and single lap joints.

Cutting sequence   Cut a rabbet across the end of the tail piece with a shoulder plane. Partially cut the tails with a dovetail saw. Remove the bulk of the waste with chisel and mallet. Finish the faces with bench chisels. Mark the pins from the tails and cut in the same way as the pin piece for a single lap dovetail. How to make a double lap dovetail is explained in Chapter 6.

Repeat performance   Making the pins for a double lap dovetail is the same as making the pins for a single lap joint. Making the tails requires a new technique.

Why make a dovetail joint you can't see? The answer is to utilize the strength of the dovetail joint and the positive positioning of the parts while the furniture is being made, plus the undeniable permanence once the glue is cured.

To make the joint more attractive in front elevation, miter the corners. If you dislike the stripe of end grain visible along one edge, mold it into a very fine bullnose or bead. It may be beaded across the end grain only, or continued round the long grain, or extended to all the outer corners. The highlights and shadows created by the bead emphasize the architecture of the piece, adding a design detail that grows naturally out of the joint.

◄ *To visualize* the pins and tails concealed inside a double lap dovetail, imagine a single lap dovetail with a pad of wood over the tail piece.

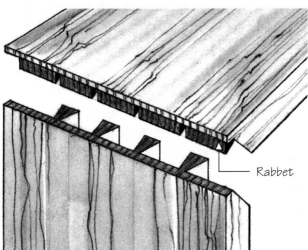

◄ *Part names* are the same as for a single lap, plus the rabbet cut on the tail piece.

Rabbet

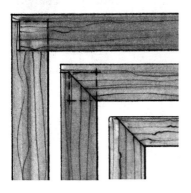

◄ *Edge view* of a double lap dovetail.
◄ *Mitered* corner double lap dovetail.
◄ *Edges* molded with a bead.

▲ *Double lap* dovetail closed.

Secret miter dovetail

The secret miter dovetail is the sophisticate of the dovetail family. It has all the strength of a through dovetail, but it's completely invisible – all you see is a mitered corner.

When you make veneered furniture you expect to let the beauty of the wood meet uninterrupted at a corner. However, the same visual argument applies to solid wood where the ego of the maker sometimes takes precedence over the good of the piece. Allowing the wood to speak for itself through the simplicity of a silent joint is often the most attractive design solution.

With material that has complex colors or a strong pattern value of its own, such as spalted maple or Macassar ebony, adding the competing pattern value of a through dovetail can be distracting. Some woods may be so dark that a through dovetail is almost invisible anyway, so choosing it for the pattern value of pins and tails is effort wasted.

The secret miter dovetail breaks the construction pattern of the previous three joints that all began with making the tail piece before pin piece. In this case, you reverse the procedure and make the pin piece *before* the tail piece.

Cutting sequence   Cut a rabbet at the end of both pieces. Mark out the pins and partially cut with a dovetail saw. Remove the bulk of the waste with chisel and mallet. Finish the surfaces with skew chisels and bench chisels powered by muscle. Mark the tails from the pins and finish the same as the pins. Miter the square edges of the rabbets, and there you have it – a dovetail incognito. How to make a secret miter dovetail is explained in Chapter 7.

Repeat performance   Apart from having to avoid sawing into the mitered rabbets on each piece, no new techniques are required.

You could use a miter with a spline, or a biscuit joint. Your decision will depend on the work in hand. For me, it's determined by the quality of the piece. If the piece has to be spot on, if it must never come apart, if the materials are the finest, the more likely I would choose to make the secret miter dovetail. No other joint can match it for strength and positive assembly of parts. When the entire piece is of the highest quality, so too should be the joinery.

◄ **To visualize** the pins and tails concealed inside a secret miter dovetail, imagine pads of wood placed on the tail piece and the pin piece of a mitered through dovetail.

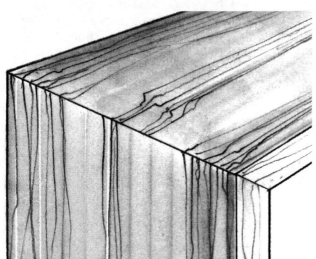

◄ **Part names** are the same as for a double lap dovetail, plus rabbets cut on the tail and pin pieces.

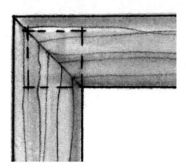

◄ **Edge view** secret miter dovetail.

Strength of a Dovetail

We know that a dovetail joint is strong, but what does that mean? A good definition of strong is "the ability to resist stress." Since examples of broken dovetail joints are rare, the joint is clearly capable of resisting stress. However, if you want recommendations for joint design based on laboratory strength testing, you're out of luck. Testing solid wood joints, such as a dovetail or a mortise and tenon, is such a complicated procedure that the results would be worthless for everyday practical applications.

For instance, to which of the various stresses would you subject the joint: compression, tensile, static bending, impact bending or torque? What species of wood would you use for the test; what was its growth rate, its moisture content? How was the joint designed, how smooth were the joining surfaces, how tight were the faces, and what glue was used? Finally, joints don't occur singly in furniture construction, they occur in groups of four or eight as part of a structure. Strength testing a joint as a guide to its design is too complex with too many variables. We must rely on experience.

Understanding joint strength

Joint strength has two components:

- joint mechanics
- glue area

Joint mechanics has two aspects:

- proportion
- accuracy of fit

Joint mechanics

Proportion   Proportion describes how much of each joint remains on the board once it's cut. For example, if the tails and pins are equal, then half the joint material is on one board and half on the other. All other factors being the same, this is the strongest form of joint – one you might expect to find in lots of old furniture. However, furniture makers long ago recognized that dovetail joints made this way were far stronger than the stresses placed upon them, so equal tails and pins are seldom seen.

An extreme pin-to-tail ratio is found in the front corner joint on the drawers made by London furniture makers in the 17th Century. Determined to create the most elegant of single lap dovetails, they designed a joint in which 10% of the material consisted of pins and 90% consisted of tails. Add the stress that opening the drawer places on the pins, which were frequently Cuban mahogany, a species not known for great strength, and you realize that these earlier makers had pushed dovetail design to the limit.

Accuracy of fit   To be tight, a joint requires accuracy of fit, that is, the two faces must be smooth and aligned with one another. "Tight" like "strong" is a slippery word. Optimum tightness is determined by defining its two extremes: too loose and the joint easily comes apart; too tight and one piece or the other splits during assembly. Somewhere between these two extremes is where you want to be be.

There are more variables. Don't forget that the joint must be glued. It's not uncommon to make a dovetail, put it together dry, and conclude the fit is appropriately tight. Then, when you apply glue and tighten the clamps, the joint splits. That's because glue not only has thickness, but most glues, being water-based, put moisture into the wood and cause it to swell. Adding glue changes a tight dry fit into an overtight wet fit.

Glue area

Glue area has two aspects:

- grain orientation

- number of glue lines

Grain orientation   When making tails and pins, you produce two types of surface: **long grain** and **end grain**. Using the through dovetail as an example, the long grain surface is the sawn face from the dovetail saw; the end grain surface is the chiseled shoulder at the bottom of the socket.

In the glued-up joint, the two surfaces form two types of interface: **long grain to long grain** (the sawn faces of tails and pins) and **long grain to end grain** (the inside faces of the tails and pins with the chiseled shoulders of tails and pins).

The long grain to long grain interface is much stronger than the long grain to end grain interface. Nonetheless, when gluing up any dovetail joint, put glue on *all* the contact faces.

Glue lines   The greater the number of glue lines, the greater the strength of the joint. That's a truism which, like the ratio of pin to tail, doesn't help a lot. We simply can't distinguish among too few, enough, and too many. We can only consider the appearance of the joint and assume that we've included enough glue lines.

The tightness of the glue line interface plays an important role in joint strength once glue is applied, but again we are unable garner information by testing. Since the joint comes straight from the saw and chisel and tightness is more art than science, our efforts become just another variable. Too tight a joint with no splitting may cause glue starvation. But as long as the joint stays together we will never know whether looser would have been stronger.

Our understanding of strength is rooted almost entirely in experience. However, we can agree that the dovetail is so strong that we can devote our attention to appearance without worrying about compromising its strength.

Designing the through dovetail

There are two major points to address in the design of the through dovetail joint:

- the **slope** or angle of the tails and pins

- the **layout** or relative size of the tails and pins

Appearance is the combined effect of slope and layout that produces a pattern of long grain and end grain – what we see of the joint.

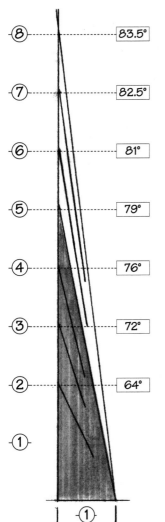

83.5°

82.5°

81°

79°

76°

72°

64°

Determining the slope

Because woodworking has no measuring tool graduated in degrees, slope is expressed as the ratio of width to length. For example, a slope of one to five is set by first drawing the length line on a board or your bench at right angles to its edge, then marking a point five inches along the line. Mark the width by making a point on the edge one inch from the length line. Join the two points and you have a slope of 1:5. Set a sliding bevel to this slope and use for marking out.

The exact slope isn't important, but there are two extremes to avoid. In my experience, it goes like this: if the line is too close to a right angle, say, a slope of 1:8 or more, there is too little dovetail effect – it looks more like a box joint gone wrong. Alternatively, a slope of 1:3 is so extreme that the elegance of the dovetail is lost. There's also a practical consideration. A slope below 1:3 creates weak short grain on the edges of the tails that is prone to breaking off as you make or fit the joint.

◀ *Seven slopes ranging from 1:2 to 1:8. Degrees are approximate and included for information only since the woodworker has no measuring tool graduated in degrees. A slope around 1:5 usually produces the best-looking dovetail.*

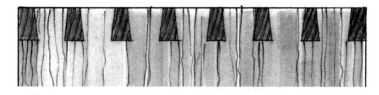

▶ *Slope 1:9*
too steep.

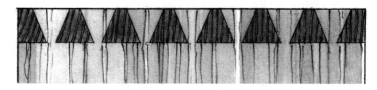

▶ *Slope 1:2*
too extreme.

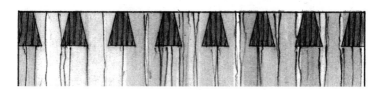

▶ *Slope 1:5*
about right.

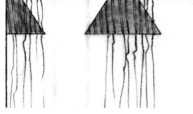

▶ *Fragile*
short grain
on tail with
less than
1:2 slope.

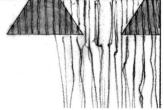

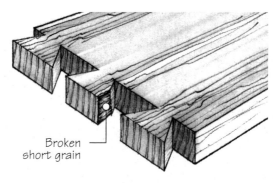

Broken
short grain

◀ *Broken*
short grain is
a danger if
the slope is
too extreme.

Most of the time, I set the sliding bevel by eye. I've kept track for a long time to see if there is any consistency in what I think is a pleasing slope. In practically every case it falls between 1:4 and 1:5. The slight variations seem related to the thickness of the wood. You can decide for yourself what looks best.

Old books often recommended that the slope should be steeper in softwood joints than in hardwood joints. This is a frivolous concern. The joint is so strong that slope is not a factor. Appearance, not strength, is your major concern.

Layout

When making furniture such as a sideboard or a chest of drawers, the tails are typically cut on the horizontal boards – the top and bottom pieces – and the pins are cut on the vertical boards – the sides. When the boards stand on edge, as in a lidded box, the tails go on on the long front and back pieces and the pins on the shorter ends. The series of paired drawings on the following pages adopt this convention.

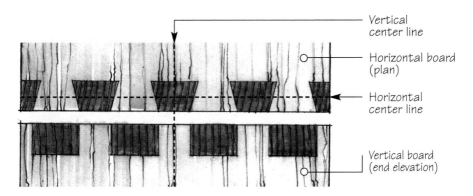

Vertical center line

Horizontal board (plan)

Horizontal center line

Vertical board (end elevation)

▲ **Key** to layout drawings. The horizontal board is shown in plan. The vertical board is shown in end elevation.

Layout design options

There are three major design options. You can:

- make the tails and pins equal
- make the tails bigger than the pins
- make the pins bigger than the tails

Tails and pins equal

Equal tails and pins is a common choice when designing your first layouts. The next decision is what size to make them. One consideration is that the smaller the size, the greater the number of glue lines. Remember, however, that appearance is much more important than strength. Furthermore, the notion of "equal" is relative rather than absolute. It depends upon how you look at the joint.

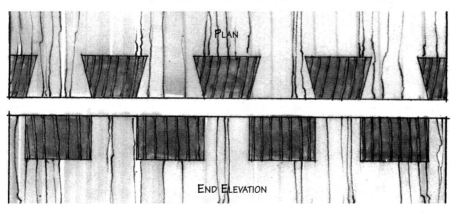

▲ **Tails and pins** are equal size in plan – the spacing is equal on the horizontal center line.

However, the size of the end grain tails in end elevation is noticeably larger than the pins.

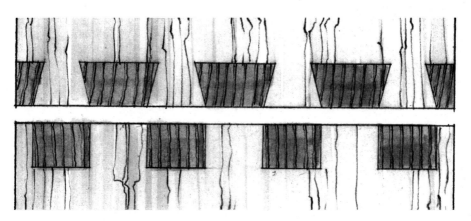

▲ **If the spacing** is equal in end elevation, the tails

become smaller than the pins when seen in plan.

Tails bigger

When either the pins or the tails dominate, the question is, To what degree is one dominant over the other? One limiting factor is how small can the pins be made? As small as the entry saw kerf between the tails.

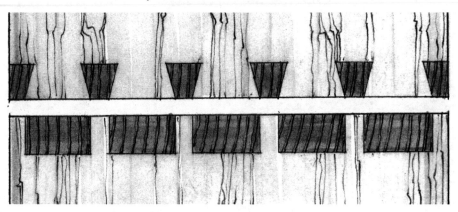

▲ *Tails bigger* layout in this instance lack visual impact.

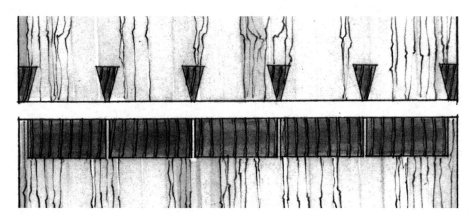

▲ *The dominance* of tails has been amplified so much in this layout that the tiny pins have a visual impact of their own.

Pins bigger

Joints made with pins bigger than tails are unusual, although I've occasionally seen this layout on country-made softwood chests. Very small tails simply lack the visual impact of very small pins.

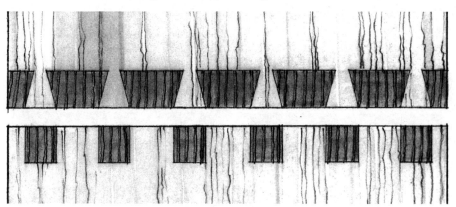

▲ **Pins bigger** layout is rare and lacks visual impact.

Varying the layout

A row of through dovetails made with same-size pins and tails is repetitive and dull. Traditionally we make the tails larger than the pins and we vary the size of the tails while keeping the size of the pins uniform.

The following layouts are not exhaustive, but they provide a good starting point for considering variations that suit your needs. At the end of the day you have to design the joint details to make it your own.

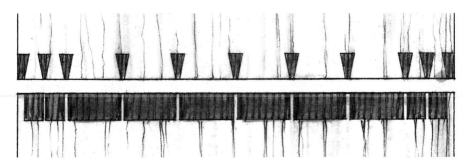

▲ **Two sizes** of tail – the outer groups serve two practical purposes. Being smaller, they create 5 glue lines each which prevent the edges of the workpiece from curling up. They also resist the stress of lifting that large structures such as sideboards are commonly subjected to when moved about.

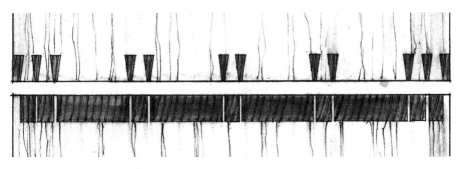

▲ **This layout** is very similar to the one above. The outer groups are the same, but in between there are twin pins with a small tail between each large tail.

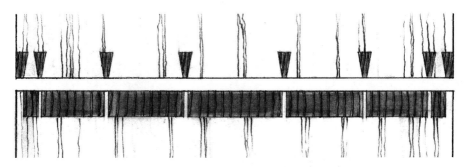

▲ **Different size** tails – the pattern is symmetrical about the vertical center line, the center tail is the largest, and the tails get smaller as they approach the edge. The change in size is more obvious on furniture seen full size.

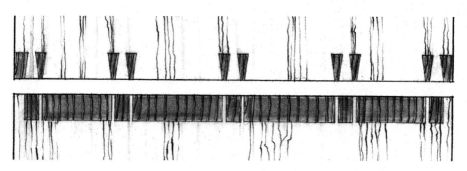

▲ **Small outer** tails are the same pattern as the small inner tails. The number of outer glue lines is reduced to 3.

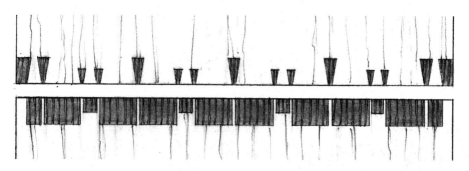

▲ **Most dramatic** of all is the "hound's tooth" layout with small dovetails placed inside larger dovetails. Here the small tails and pins are cut to the halfway point on both the horizontal and vertical boards.

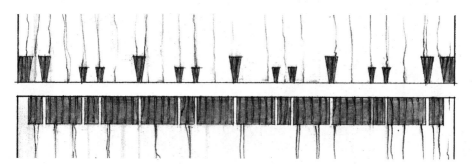

▲ **In this hound's tooth** variation, the tail socket is cut to common shoulder line on the vertical board, presenting the pins as a series of strong fine vertical lines.

Outer Edges

Tail first or pin first

The lines of the outer edges of the joint will be affected by whether you begin with a tail or a pin. Actually, it's a half tail or a half pin because the outer edge is straight – it can't be "dovetailed." Half pins and half tails are prone to splitting off if the joint faces are too tight.

For my own work I always begin with a half pin because I consider a whole tail at the outer edge more attractive. On a case piece, your decision determines whether the outer edge of the side runs through like a column or the outer edge of the top runs through like a transom. There is no technical reason to prefer one over the other.

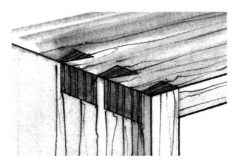

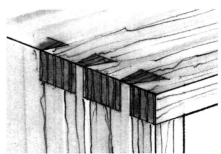

▲ *Half pin* on outer edge.

▲ *Half tail* on outer edge.

Mitered shoulder

It's worth the trouble to miter the corners of a through dovetail. A mitered corner unifies the parts, making a strong connection between the sides and top. You still have to decide whether to begin the joint with a tail or a pin.

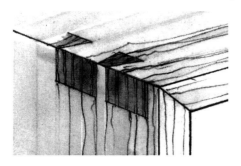

▲ *Half pin* on outer edge, with mitered corner.

▲ *Half tail* on outer edge, with mitered corner.

Simplifying marking layouts

First attempts at laying out dovetails directly onto the wood all too often result in errors that have to be erased and redrawn. Repeated remarking leads to a confusion so complete that planing the surface clean and starting again is the only solution.

If you're not confident about laying out the joint on the end grain of the tail piece, do a paper layout, using the following step-by-step procedure. It clarifies the connection between the sloping line layout on the face of the work and the squared lines on the end grain. It also allows you to rework a solution without mess. With experience, you will lay out directly on the workpiece.

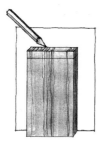 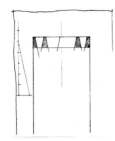 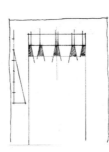 

1 *Set a cutting gauge to about 1/32" less than the thickness of the tail piece and mark around the ends of both pieces.*

2 *Make a full size drawing by tracing the outline of the tail piece onto a pad of paper.*

3 *Draw a line corresponding to the gauge line on the tail piece, 1/32 in. less than the thickness of the wood.*

4 *Mark a vertical center line to help maintain balance. Draw a slope for reference. Shade the pins to visualize the joint better.*

5 *Draw a second line 5/8" above your drawing and square lines across at the intersection of the slopes. This represents the end grain of the tail piece.*

6 *Cut the drawing from the sheet and fold it along the middle line, which represents the edge of the end grain.*

7 *Attach the drawing to the tail piece with clear tape. Using an awl, sharp pen, or pocket knife, mark points on the lines crossing the end grain.*

8 *Remove paper and square across the marked points with a sharp pencil. Set a sliding bevel and mark the slope of the tails.*

CHAPTER 2

Tools – selection and preparation

You don't need a lot of tools to make dovetail joints by hand. However, with the exception of measuring tools, you must expect to make minor adjustments to your woodworking tools as they come from the box. How to do so is explained here.

If your toolbox is empty or minus a few items, this chapter will help you assess what must be bought. If you have some or all of the tools, you can determine if any need improvement or replacement.

The tools are divided into four groups:

Marking tools
- pencils
- marking knife

Measuring & marking tool
- cutting gauge

Measuring tools
- try square
- miter square
- sliding bevel
- rule
- straight edge
- winding sticks

Cutting tools
- dovetail saw
- coping saw
- bevel-edged chisels
- bench plane
- shoulder plane

Marking tools

pencils, marking knife

Marks are divided into two categories:

- surface lines, made by pencil
- incised lines, made by knife

Surface lines

The most universal marking tool is the pencil. It makes two specific types of mark:

- orientation marks
- cutting guidelines

Orientation Marks

Orientation marks record the face side and the face edge, which in turn tells you what part goes where in the work, which face is in or out, and which edge is up or down. They also record which piece is 1, 2, 3 or 4. When making dovetails, orientation marks tell you the inside faces. Marking is explained in detail in Chapter 3, *Preparation of Stock,* page 51.

Because marks tend to get smudged and worn as the work proceeds, make them boldly with a soft pencil. A 4B works well. Later, during the cleaning up process, it's easy to remove orientation marks. One pass with a plane – the removal of one thin shaving – and the mark is gone.

◄ *Orientation marks tell you how and where to place the piece in the work.*

Cutting guidelines

A cutting guideline tells you where to cut. On the tail piece of a through dovetail, the pencil guidelines on the end grain tell you where to saw at right angles to the face of the wood. Guidelines down the face tell you where to saw a straight sloping line. Use a sharp B pencil – and keep it sharp.

Incised lines

Made by knife and cutting gauge, incised lines are intended to be cut. They are more precise and definitive than pencil marks and they remain until the work is finished.

You use a marking knife to mark the slope of the pins on the end grain by using the tails as a template. Pencil guidelines tell you where the vertical plane lies.

The surface tissues incised by your marking knife and cutting gauge form the visible edge or shoulder of the joint. Half of the incised line remains after the shoulder is made. One side of the mark you make at the outset is what you will see at the end.

Incised lines form the perfect guide for positioning the edge of a chisel when cutting a shoulder.

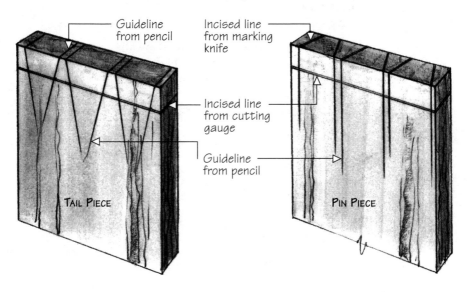

Guideline from pencil

Incised line from marking knife

Incised line from cutting gauge

Guideline from pencil

TAIL PIECE

PIN PIECE

▲ *Examples* of surface lines and incised lines typically marked on a dovetail tail piece.

The blade of a marking knife should be thin in section and sharpened to a slim V. In side elevation the end of the knife should be rounded rather than pointed. A pointed knife is liable to produce a ragged cut because of the pressure concentrated at the point. A rounded knife, with pressure distributed over a curved edge, will produce a smooth cut. The stiffness of the blade is also important – too thin and it bends under pressure; too thick and it's difficult to place the cutting edge exactly into the corner between the try square blade and the wood.

▲ **The blade** of a marking knife must be thin in section, sharpened to a very slim V, and stiff enough not to bend under pressure.

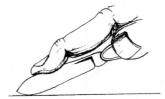

▲ **A rounded knife** produces a smooth cut because pressure is distributed over a curved edge rather than concentrated at the point.

Most quality pocket knives can be modified to perform as a marking knife. The knife that fits the bill perfectly for me is a two-blade Swiss Army knife.

The "traditional" marking knife (also called a striking knife from "striking" a line) in fact has no tradition. It's a manufactured version of a tool that woodworkers once commonly made for themselves. The manufactured version is flat on one face and sharpened on the other, like a chisel.

Measuring & marking tool

cutting gauge

Cutting gauge

Of the three gauges in the woodworker's toolkit – marking gauge, mortise gauge, and cutting gauge – only the cutting gauge is required for marking out dovetail joints. It has three major parts: the wooden fence, the stock, and the metal knife that makes the mark.

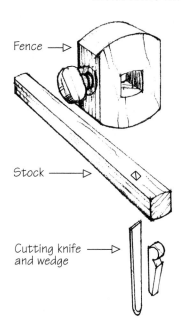

Fence ⟶▷

Stock ⟶▷

Cutting knife
and wedge ⟶▷

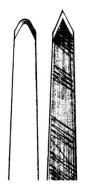

A gauge line can only be as accurate as the face that guides the fence. The cutting gauge marks the length of the tails and pins of the dovetail joint, so it works off the end grain and cuts a line across the grain. The first step therefore is to prepare the ends of the boards to the level of accuracy that you want transmitted into the joint.

Don't substitute a marking gauge with a cutting gauge: they are *not* interchangeable. The marking gauge is designed to cut with the grain. If you use it to mark across the grain, its spur produces torn fibers and no usable mark.

Sharpening the knife   The knife of the cutting gauge produces a clean, crisp cut across the grain – provided it is properly profiled and sharpened. The knife prepared by most manufacturers is sharpened to a point, but the gauge works better with a semicircular cutting end, beveled on one side only.

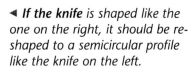

◄ *If the knife* is shaped like the one on the right, it should be reshaped to a semicircular profile like the knife on the left.

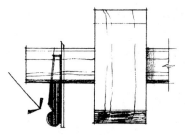

◄ *Remove* the brass wedge by tapping downward with a small hammer or niggling with your fingers.

Release the knife by removing the brass wedge. Make the semicircular profile on the grinding wheel first, then grind to a 25° sharpening angle. Complete the sharpening on a stone and back off as you would a chisel. Because there is so little metal to remove, do the whole operation with a light touch.

Placing the knife   You can insert the knife with its flat side toward the fence or away from it. It depends upon which side of the knife line is the waste side. Place the knife so the tissue crushed by the knife bevel lies on the waste side. When marking out dovetails, the flat side faces away from the fence.

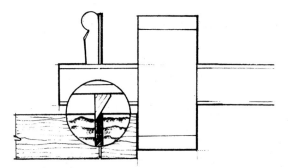

◄ *When marking* out the shoulder line for dovetails, the waste side of the knife line is toward the fence which rides on the end grain of the workpiece. The flat side of the knife faces away from the fence.

Looks are deceiving   Expensive gauges feature two brass strips let into the face of the fence. Manufacturers claim that the brass retards wear. Although the inlays add an air of quality, they hinder accurate measurement because they invariably stand proud of the surface when the wood shrinks or as a result of sanding during manufacture. Place a straight edge across the inlays to assess the extent of the hollowing. Avoid potential problems by avoiding the inlays, either by reversing the fence and using its opposite side, or by removing the inlays and re-facing the fence with a light-colored, dense hardwood.

Measuring tools

sliding bevel, miter square,
try square, rule, straightedge, winding strips

Sliding bevel

Use the sliding bevel for setting out and verifying slopes. The tool consists of a stock and a moveable slotted metal blade, which is locked in position by a wing-nut or a lever. Though the old-style wood-and-metal model is attractive, an all-metal tool is more accurate. The pivot end is shaped like a rule joint and the point where flatness stops – at right angles from the pivot pin – is clearly defined. Also, its locking mechanism is usually located in the heel of the stock, well away from the marking operation.

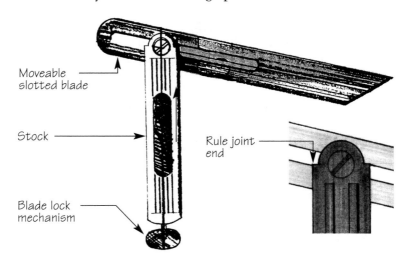

Moveable slotted blade

Stock

Rule joint end

Blade lock mechanism

Miter square

You need a miter square to mark out the miter on the edge of a through dovetail joint. I prefer the Japanese model, which is a 45° parallelogram with a fence along one edge, though it suffers from not having an internal 45° angle for checking a miter once cut. Check the cut miter with a combination square.

Try square

The try square is used constantly when measuring and marking out. It measures 90° when you are checking for square. It establishes a 90° line when you mark out with knife or pencil.

Four types are available:

- wood stock with fixed metal blade
- machinist's square
- double-sided square
- combination square

To be accurate, the blade and the stock must each have parallel faces and the two parts must be joined at 90°.

Any of these four will do the job, though as with the cutting gauge and the sliding bevel, combining wood and metal is potentially troublesome. For dovetail-making I prefer the double-sided square. Because it measures distance and right angularity, it's a big improvement on options one and two. A knurled nut in the center of the stock locks the sliding, graduated blade. I use the 4-inch (100mm) and 6-inch (150mm) models constantly.

Rule

You will collect a variety of rules. Since most woodworking less than an inch is measured in eighths or parts of an eighth, get an easy-to-see 12-inch rule graduated in sixteenths. Marks down to 32nds are seldom necessary. A six-inch rule is also useful. Most of the time I use the blade from one of my try squares.

Straightedge

You may have avoided buying a straightedge because it is expensive and because its usefulness is unclear. However, when preparing your first piece of stock you will realize that the only way to check it for flatness in length is with a straightedge.

Buy the best metal straightedge from companies which specialize in the manufacture of measuring tools. The edge accuracy of .0005 in. doesn't indicate the standard required for woodworking so much as reflect the high standard to which the tool is made. A good working size ranges 18 to 24 in.

(450–600mm). Over 36 in. (900mm) long the tool becomes cumbersome for most bench work, but is a superb instrument for checking furniture assemblies and machine tables.

All tools deserve respect, but the straightedge requires special care. Once its highly accurate edge is damaged, it's simply another piece of metal. Never use its edge as a knife guide for cutting veneers or leather. A sharp knife will actually remove a very thin shaving of metal. After a few knife strokes the edge is ruined.

Winding strips

Despite being the only measuring tools we have for checking twist, winding strips are not found in woodworking tool catalogs. Like apprentices in an earlier age, you have to make your own. The drawing shows the dimensions of a typical set of winding strips 10 in. (250mm) long. This is a good general size, but furniture makers need shorter ones for edges and much longer ones for assembled furniture. Three sets are not uncommon. Use one set to check the accuracy of another.

Old-time winding strips commonly had an inlay of holly or ivory at each end of the back strip. The white spots contrasted sharply above the front strip inlaid with ebony along its top edge. The center marks were often detailed with inlay or incised carving.

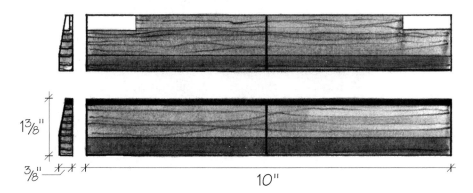

1³⁄₈"

³⁄₈"

10"

Winding strips are easy to use. Place one strip at right angles to the edge of the workpiece and as near one end as possible. Sight the top edges by aligning your eyes with the two center marks. Because the workpiece may vary in twist from end to end, place the second strip on center and check for twist in one half of the board. Repeat the procedure on the other half.

Cutting tools
dovetail saw, coping saw, chisels, bench plane, shoulder plane

West meets East

To saw the fine joints required for dovetail joinery, you need a saw with several qualities. To minimize the kerf, the blade must be thin but stiff. To produce an accurate sawn face, the teeth must be small, numerous, and sharp. Two kinds of saw have evolved with these characteristics. In the West, it's the European dovetail saw; in the East, it's the Japanese dozuki saw. Using either kind, you can produce a joint which fits directly from the saw. From now on I'll refer to the Western saw as a dovetail saw and the Eastern saw as a dozuki saw.

Dovetail saw

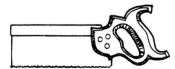

The dovetail saw has a folded metal strip on the top edge or back of the blade. The strip, made of brass or steel, stiffens the blade so it won't flex on the push stroke.

The saw is 8 to 9 in. (200–225mm) long and has a very thin blade with 18–20 points per inch (ppi). Beginning woodworkers are tempted to use it for cutting all "fine" joints, especially tenons. In practice, the dovetail saw tends to wander from the line in hard wood larger than 1 in. × 1 in. (25mm × 25mm) in section. This is a tool to be precious about. Reserve it strictly for dovetails – it's too delicate for general sawing.

The teeth are sprung set, which means they are bent about half-way down their length, alternating left and right. The set produces a kerf about 1½ times the thickness of the blade. A debate continues... should the tooth profile be cross-cut or rip? Since tail cuts and pin cuts are so short and thus relatively quick to make, cutting speed is irrelevant. What matters is that the saw will hold the line. Either a cross-cut or rip profile will do that – provided the teeth are sharp. If your saw cuts slowly or wanders, don't blame the profile, sharpen the teeth.

Two types of handle are available, D-handle or pistol-grip.

Gent's saw   The gent's saw is a variation of the dovetail saw. It's made in several sizes, from 4 in. to 9 in. (100–225mm) long. The shorter, thinner blades have up to 30 ppi, and the larger thicker blades have a ppi range of 16–20. The finer saws are useful for cutting inlays, bandings, and small moldings. I've known many furnituremakers who prefer it to its larger cousin.

Buying a dovetail saw

Time was when the choice of makers was large and quality of saws was high. You could expect to use the tool straight from the box. That's not the way it works now. Increasingly, the best tools are sold by makers or vendors who specialize in only a few tools, but ones they guarantee will work. You will undoubtedly pay more for such assurance, but the price is worth it.

Dozuki saw

Because the dozuki saw cuts on the pull stroke, it's able to obtain sufficient stiffness with a thinner blade and so produces a thinner kerf.

It's available in several lengths, ranging from 7 in. to 10 in. (175–250mm), measured along the cutting edge. The teeth are long and fine and the ppi range is 18–24.

The blade tapers towards the handle, which will probably require a slight adjustment in technique for someone accustomed to a dovetail saw in which tooth edge and back edge are parallel. And because it cuts on the pull stroke, it obscures the pencil and knife lines with sawdust, which you will have to blow away as the sawcut proceeds.

Coping saw

This saw takes its name from the practice of coping a molding. A molding is coped when its end grain is profiled to fit over the face of an adjacent molding. Having a very narrow blade, the saw is well-suited to cutting the tight curves required by coping, although you seldom use it for that purpose today. However, it's the ideal tool for removing the bulk waste in a through dovetail.

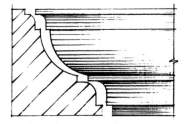

▲ **Before** power tools, the coping saw was the only convenient way to cope or profile the end of a molding.

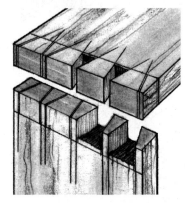

◄ *The narrow blade of a coping saw is well suited for removing the waste between tails and pins.*

The saw consists of a metal U-shaped frame made of flat steel bar, a handle, and a blade. The frame opening is smaller than the length of the blade. You compress the frame to fit the blade. When released, the frame expands and holds the blade in tension. Insert the blade with the teeth pointing towards the handle so the saw cuts on the pull stroke.

▲ ►*Moveable spigot and tapered pins allow blade to be locked in the frame at various angles.*

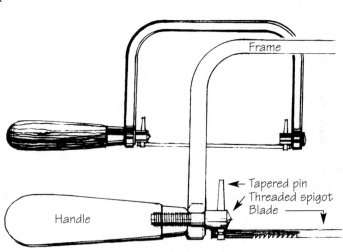

Frame

← Tapered pin
Threaded spigot
Blade

Handle

Chisels

Chisels were once available in a wide variety of types and names, mostly associated with handles. All that matters is the shape of the section through the blade. It is either rectangular, which is called a firmer chisel, or rectangular with corners removed, which is called a bevel-edged firmer chisel. You need a bevel-edged chisel for dovetail work because its shape enables you to cut into the corners of the joint. You have three types to choose from, distinguished chiefly by blade length:

- patternmaker's chisel, 9 in. (225mm)
- bevel-edged firmer, 6 in. (150mm)
- Japanese chisel, 2 in. (50mm)

Since there is no technical advantage of one blade length over the other, the choice is yours.

Chisels are available in a variety of widths, from 1/4 in. (6mm) to 1 in. (25mm), in 1/8 (3mm) increments. Because you need a variety of widths and because chisels are relatively inexpensive, it's a false economy to avoid buying a complete range.

Sharpening a chisel

New chisels don't come ready for work. You must polish and sharpen them to get the razor edge necessary for driving a chisel through wood by hand power. The following steps may also be necessary for your old chisels.

Polish the back on a succession of flat sharpening stones, working from coarse to ultrafine. Sharpening is a two-step procedure. First, using a power grinder, make a 20° grinding bevel on the side opposite the polished flat face. Second, using stones medium to ultrafine, make a 30° sharpening bevel. How to sharpen chisels and plane irons is explained in detail in my book *Sharpening with Waterstones*.

To prevent a nasty cut when using a new chisel, remove the sharp corner where the flat back meets the long edge. A few strokes on a medium stone with the flat back held at 45° will do the job.

Skew chisels To clean out the sockets of a single lap, a double lap, or a secret miter dovetail, you need two skew chisels. Make them from a pair of 1/4 in. (6mm) bevel-edged chisels ground and sharpened to an angle you typically use on your dovetails. Shape one chisel to work the left side of the socket; shape the other to work the right side. Make the chisel angle 3° to 5° more acute than the socket angle.

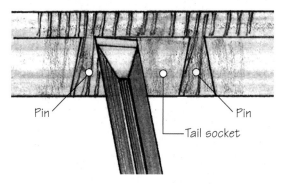

◄ *Purpose-made* skew chisels let you pare the corners of a tail socket.

Pin

Pin

Tail socket

To make a skew chisel, first shape the end to the desired skew angle.Hold the chisel at a radius to the wheel on a tool rest, flat side down. This makes the cutting end flat. Next shape the grinding bevel. If you try to shape and make the grinding bevel at the same time, you will create a feather edge and burn the steel. Finish by sharpening.

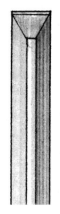

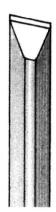

▲ *A 1/4 in. (6mm) bevel-edged firmer.*

▲ *Grind the skew angle.*

▲ *Make a 20° grinding bevel.*

▲ *Make a 30° sharpening bevel.*

Bench planes

You may choose to use a bench plane instead of a chop saw to square the ends of material and to make parts to length prior to marking out the dovetail. Keep in mind, however, that the bench plane has a range of uses so diverse that makes it unique among hand tools and machines. You can use it from start to finish in making a piece of furniture: at the preparation stage to true the parts of the work, at the subassembly stage to align and true assemblies, at the fitting stage to shoot drawers and fit doors, and at the end of the job to prepare the outside surfaces for the final finish.

Correctly tuned and sharpened, the bench plane does three things:

- dimensions material to a given size
- creates flatness on a twisted surface or a twisted assembly
- smooths a surface in preparation for the final finish

Although the sizing and naming of planes is not standardized, they can be loosely categorized by manufacturers' numbers that are usually cut into the body and by historic names.

The longest bench planes made were 24 in. (600mm) long, the shortest 5 in. (125mm). The longest was numbered #8 or #08, depending on the maker, the smallest was #3 or #03, and there was a size for every number in between. The longer planes are called trying or shooting planes, the shorter ones are called smoothing planes, and the ones in between are called jack planes.

The longer the plane, the longer the piece of wood it will plane flat. Throughout my working life I have used only two planes, a 22 in. (550mm) #07 and a 9 in. (225mm)#04½. If your trying plane and smoothing plane are the same width, you have the added advantage of interchangeable blades.

Shoulder plane

When making a double lap dovetail or a secret miter dovetail, you begin by cutting a rabbet with a shoulder plane.

Once widely produced, shoulder planes are now available from a handful of small tool companies. You could also search for a used one.

Three different sizes are available. Since all work equally well, choose the size and weight that suits you best. As with all low-angle planes, the blade has no cap iron and it sits with the flat side to the frog. Sharpen it at the same angle as a bench plane.

The blade is made fractionally wider than the sole. You must therefore move the blade left or right make it flush with the side of the tool that is cutting the rabbet. To eliminate the fuss of adjustment, you can grind the blade width equal to the sole width, but don't make it less because a narrow blade is awkward to reposition each time you work from the opposite side of the plane.

Aids and recommendations

Magnifying your work

To improve as a woodworker, there's nothing like seeing your mistakes clearly. That's why I stress the importance of magnifying lenses. When you magnify saw kerf and knife line, you see exactly how the tissue collapses as the cut approaches a critical stopping point. When joint lines and sawn faces are seen large, you can clearly see what must be done to make things better. Your choices include a hand lens, a magnifying lamp, and a binocular magnifier.

Hand lens

A hand lens four inches in diameter with a magnification power up to 4 works well. The hand lens should be on your bench most of the time, and easily available when not.

Magnifying lamp

For a clear, well-lit, hands-free view of cutting and paring in progress, consider a bench-mounted magnifying lamp. Typical features include an arm with a three-foot reach and a magnification power of 1.75.

Binocular magnifier

A binocular magnifier also allows you to work with both hands free. Features include an adjustable headband, a tilt-up lens frame that will fit over glasses, and a magnification power of 1.75 or 2.75.

Quick and accurate vise work

The following recommendations are techniques rather than tools. I include them because they make tools easier to use.

Vertical mounting   To quickly locate the workpiece vertically in the vise, mark the vise cheek and the bench top with a pencil or knife line taken from the outside edge of the vise support bar. Now, when you place the workpiece tight to the support bar and aligned with the pencil or knife line, it's bound to be vertical – if the bench top is horizontal and the vise is properly mounted.

To mark the line, put the stock of the try square on the top edge of the fixed cheek and run the top edge of the blade up against the support bar. Pencil or knife a line on the cheek at this point, across the edge, and continue the line an inch or so along the bench top.

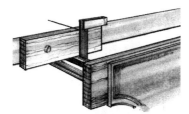

◄ *Vertical mounting – square a line across the vise cheek, cheek edge, and part of the bench top to help you quickly position the workpiece vertically.*

Horizontal mounting   To make the shoulder line edge cuts with saw and chisel, the work is mounted horizontally in the vise. Regardless of how high out of the vise you want the work, first trap it between the open vise jaws by tilting the top edge away from you. As you tighten the vise, ensure parallelism by sighting the top edge with a line on the bench surface. My bench top is made of laminated strips so there is no shortage of sight lines. Draw a line if necessary.

◄ *Horizontal mounting – trap the workpiece between the vise jaws and sight the top edge with a line on the bench top.*

CHAPTER 3

Putting the tools to work

The best way to learn to make a dovetail joint – or any other joint – is to break it down into its various parts and practice making the relevant cuts until they come from saw, chisel, and plane with ease and accuracy. This is how apprentices of old learned their trade – by making bits and pieces rather than entire projects.

If you are tempted to follow the "I want to make a project" route, struggling with the how-to as you proceed, I offer the following cautions. Your attention is misplaced: it's focused on the finished item rather than on how to correctly use the tools required to make it. Anxious to get the job done, you make mistakes and frustration mounts. In the end you shrug off shoddy work by saying, "Oh well, I'll get it right next time."

The importance of practice

Don't begin learning about woodworking by making complete joints that are essential to a project that you promised to have completed in three days. Start by making what the tool makes: learn to use a plane by making shavings, how to use a saw by making sawdust, and how to use a chisel by making chips. And when you can make good shavings, good sawdust and good chips, then you are ready to make good joints.

How much time you devote to learning woodworking will vary according to ability, aspiration, and discipline. But clearly, the more you practice the fundamentals, the better the result when applied to a serious piece of furniture. The same approach is followed by the novice potter who throws a hundred pots and returns them all to the wet bin or the novice golfer who hits a thousand balls off the tee at a driving range.

Preparation of stock

Before you can begin to mark out and cut the joints when making a piece of solid wood furniture, you "prepare the stock." You begin by assembling all the parts recorded on your cutting list. Each piece of wood is in a rough state, that is, it may have been cut from a sawn board, it's not square, and its dimensions are oversize. To be useful, it must be prepared to the following conditions:

- the faces of each piece are made flat and square to each other

- each piece is cut to dimension

Because neither practice joint nor future project can be successful if this initial step is not carried out correctly, I've outlined the procedure. It's the same whether you choose to work with hand tools or machines or a combination of both.

Every piece of wood has six faces: four sides and two ends. All six have to be "made right", that is, the faces must be flat and square to each other. All the tools used in the subsequent operations of joint-making and assembly of parts are designed and built only to work safely and accurately with wood that is flat and square.

Face side (first face)

If the wood is approximately square in section, like a leg, it doesn't matter which side you begin with. If the wood is rectangular in section, you begin with one of the wide faces. First, study the piece as a whole. One of these faces is likely to be more attractive than the other. That's the side you want facing out. You start by preparing the *opposite* face – the one that is less attractive. Once this less attractive inside face is prepared, it becomes the face side and serves as a reference for subsequent operations.

By hand, use a hand plane to make this face flat. By machine, use a jointer. To confirm the flatness of the face, measure it to confirm that it is: flat along its length; flat across its width; and out of twist (winding).

You measure the first two conditions with a straight edge. You measure the third with winding sticks. A board can appear to measure flat in length and width and still be twisted.

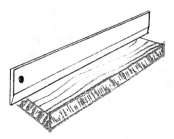 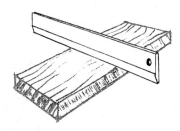

1 *Straight edge* confirms first face is flat in length.

2 *Straight edge* confirms first face is flat in width.

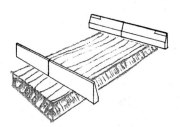

3 *Winding sticks* confirm first face is out of twist.

When this first face satisfies all three conditions for flatness, it's ready for marking with a bold looped line to identify it as the face side. But before making the mark, study the piece of wood again and decide which way it will be joined to its fellows. Which edge do you want up or down if the face is vertical or which edge do you want front or back if the face is horizontal. Hold the piece in the attitude it will assume in the assembly. If the face is vertical, draw the loop so that it exits the bottom edge. If the face is horizontal, draw it exiting the back edge. From now on this face is called the **face side**. The indicated bottom edge or back edge will become the face edge.

Face edge (second face)

Make the face edge with a hand plane or machine jointer with the fence set square. To confirm that your cutting is accurate, repeat the three checks that you did for the face side. A fourth check confirms that the face edge is square to the face side. Check with a try square.

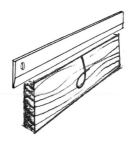

1 *Straight edge* confirms second face is flat in length.

2 *Straight edge* confirms second face is flat in width.

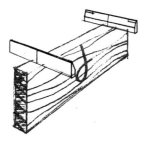

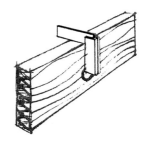

3 *Winding strips* confirm second face is out of twist.

4 *Try square* confirms second face is square to face side.

When all is correct, mark the edge with an inverted ∨. The point of the ∧ connects to the exit point of the face side mark. From now on this edge is called the **face edge**.

You still have four more faces to prepare – two sides and two ends. But first let's consider what you have already accomplished.

- you have prepared two faces that are geometrically accurate

- you have determined the orientation of the piece in the assembly

Geometric accuracy

Face sides and face edges act as reference surfaces for all sub-sequent measurements.

When marking out with hand tools – knife and square, marking gauge, rule and pencil – work from the face side or face edge as your fence. When cutting by machine, always place the face side or face edge against the machine bed or fence.

◄ *All marking* out begins from a reference surface – *either a face side or a face edge. Here the stock of the try square is placed against the face edge of the workpiece in preparation for knifing a line.*

Orientation of parts

Face sides and face edges organize the arrangement of parts.

Because the face side goes inside and the face edge goes downward or to the back side of the assembly, you have determined exactly how a particular part sits in the total assembly of pieces. There is no simpler or more effective way to organize the parts of keep track of what goes where.

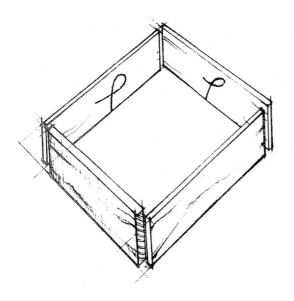

◄ *Face side* and face edge marks orient the parts in the assembly.

As for the four remaining faces, you make them accurate to the first two, but you don't mark them in any way. Now, on to the next step.

Width (third face)

Because it's always easier to saw than plane, a piece that is wider than the finished dimension by more than a saw kerf is first sawn to width. By hand, gauge to width, saw, then plane. By machine, saw to within 1/16 in., then pass through a thickness planer. You can pass several pieces of the same thickness at the same time. Check for flat, out of winding, square, and move on.

Thickness (fourth face)

By hand, gauge to thickness, then plane to the line. By machine, pass the work through a thickness planer. Check for flat, out of winding, square, and move on.

First end (fifth face)

By hand, square round the board, then plane to the line, making the end square to the face side and the face edge. By machine, it will depend on your equipment. Use a crosscut or miter fence on a table saw or a chop saw.

Second end (sixth face)

You have to do two things with the second end: get it square and get it to length. The tools and methods are the same as for the first end.

That completes preparation of the first board. The demands for the second board are even higher. Not only must must you get it square, you must get it to exactly the same length as the first board.

Summary of cuts

Operation	Cutting Tools		Measuring/Marking Tools
	Hand	*Machine*	

1 face side	trying plane	jointer	straightedge, winding sticks

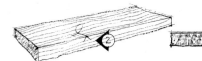

2 face edge	plane	jointer & fence	straightedge, winding sticks, try square

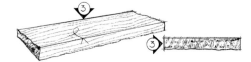

3 width	ripsaw, plane	table saw thickness planer	marking or panel gauge winding sticks, try square

4 thickness	ripsaw, plane	thickness planer	straightedge, winding sticks, marking gauge

5 first end	crosscut saw, plane	chop saw table saw	marking knife, try square

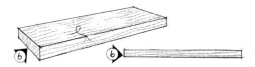

6 second end	crosscut saw, plane	chop saw table saw	rule, marking knife, try square

Dovetail logic

Accuracy and working methods

Solid wood furniture falls into two broad family groups:

- rail furniture

- case goods

Rail furniture

Rail furniture, in which legs and rails form chairs, tables, and beds, is generally joined together using some version of mortise and tenon.

Case goods

Case goods, which are enclosures to hold or store things, have doors and drawers. You can make case goods of flat boards joined at the corners with some form of dovetail joint or as a series of frames and panels. Since this book is about dovetails, it deals mainly with flat boards joined at the corners.

The accuracy of a piece of furniture depends upon the accuracy of its joinery, which in turn depends upon accurate shoulder lines. The method of establishing shoulder lines on dovetail joints differs from the method for mortise and tenon joints. Understanding one method of marking out will help you better understand the other.

Mortise and tenon shoulder lines

Imagine you are making a simple square four-legged, four-rail table. On the cutting list, the rail length includes material for the tenons at each end. On the working drawing, the distance between shoulders is clearly stated. You mark the first shoulder line by measuring the length of the tenon from the end of the rail, then squaring round using try square and marking knife. Next measure off the distance between shoulders and square round the second shoulder line with try square and marking knife. This first rail is the measuring stick used to measure and mark out all subsequent rails of the same length. Accuracy of the between shoulder measurement determines the accuracy of the piece. Neither the end of the rails nor the length of the tenons are factors.

Dovetail shoulder lines

When you make a dovetailed box or drawer, the important dimension is the overall length of the parts, not the between shoulders distance. You prepare opposite sides to the same length and square the ends. Then you mark the dovetail shoulder line with a cutting gauge riding on the end grain of the sides. Accuracy is determined by the ends of each piece and the length of the sides.

Setting the gauge

When marking the dovetail shoulder lines, the first question is, Where to set the gauge? The three options are illustrated below.

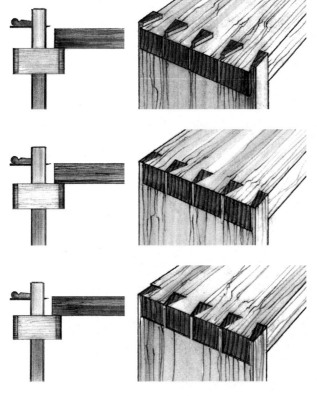

1 If you set the gauge greater than the thickness of the wood, the ends of the tails and pins will stick out above the surface of the box.

2 If you set the gauge equal to the thickness as the wood, the ends of the joints will be flush with the surface of the box.

3 If you set the gauge less than the thickness of the wood, the ends of the joints will fall short of the surface of the box.

Option 3 is the gauge setting to use. Here's why. To clean up the box, you must hand plane it to remove machine marks and dirt. The end grain of the joints, which you made exactly to length and square, are reference surfaces that now show how much to plane off each board. When you plane to the end grain at each end of a side, and a straight edge shows flatness between the two sets of end grain, then that outside face is parallel to the inside face. Each side will also be the same thickness as the other three sides. However, if you were to continue planing and remove the original end grain, you would also remove the reference surface. You would no longer know where you are in terms of thickness of that side.

With option 3, you can accomplish three important steps:

1   clean the surface by removing dirt and machine marks

2   remove the marking out lines

3   make all sides parallel and the same thickness

Options 1 and 2 are unsuitable because each obliges you to plane away the reference surface when making the joints flush and cleaning up the box. You have removed all sign-posts to accuracy. You cannot tell how big the box will be.

In the age of hand tools, the workman didn't thickness the sides of a case before assembly. He set the cutting gauge to a bit less than the thinnest part of any side, made the joints, then thicknessed its sides in the cleaning up process.

Another advantage of Option 3 is that when you glue up, you can clamp directly on the tail at each end of the box, close the joint, and move on. No need to make and position odd-shaped clamping blocks.

Hand-made drawers

The elegance of Option 3 as a working method becomes clearer when making a hand-made drawer. Start by making the front and back fit the opening. When marking out the shoulder lines, set the gauge to less than the thickness of the sides. After the joints are made and the drawer is glued together, it won't fit the opening until you plane down the sides to the end grain of the joints on the front and the back. When the plane touches the end grain, the drawer will be a perfect fit. It's a cleaning up and sizing operation all in one step.

Using the tools

The remainder of this chapter is devoted to using the tools described in Chapter 2. You will mark and make all the cuts required to make any of the four dovetail joints. Each step is fully described, plus I have included a number of exercises to enable you to focus on a particular aspect of joint making. Repeat each exercise until you can do it perfectly. You'll then be ready to make a complete joint – and you'll be delighted by how easy it is and how fine it looks.

Select practice woods

Good materials encourage good results. This applies as strongly to practice woods as to furniture stock. Invest in good practice materials and you will learn faster and enjoy it more. So avoid cutoffs lying about the shop unless they can be safely prepared to the recommended dimensions and have the recommended hardness.

Oak, cherry, maple, and ash are too hard as starters. So too is walnut, plus its color makes it difficult to gauge your progress. Pine and poplar are soft enough for sawing, but they tend to crumble when chiseled across the end grain.

I recommend Honduras mahogany. If you can find it quarter-sawn, so much the better. Butternut, basswood, and sassafras are also good choices, though they may be harder to find.

Prepare the pieces

Prepare two pieces 18 in. × 5 in. × 3/4 in. (450mm × 125mm × 19mm). If this is your debut using a handsaw, thickness down to 5/8 in. (16mm). The 1/16 in. (1.5mm) reduction in thickness makes a difference when you're starting out. As you practice, use all four ends, then cut off the practice cuts about 1/4 in. (6mm) beyond the shoulder line and start all over again. Save and number these cutoffs to record your progress.

Square the ends

Squaring the ends is Steps 5 and 6 in the preparation of stock. If you can get a spot-on result with a cross-cut box on a table saw or a chop saw, go for it. That way you remain focused on the main objective – learning to cut with saw and chisel. If you want to practice squaring the ends with a bench plane, read on. Even if you plan to square the ends by machine, you should read the sections on the marking knife and try square.

Marking knife

Grip The marking knife grip is similar to a handshake, except you place your index finger on top of the blade. The grip enables you to control downward pressure and present any part of the cutting edge to the work.

Place the knife against the blade of the try square. Align the horizontal plane of the blade with the direction of the cut. Angle the vertical plane of the blade a couple of degrees short of 90° so that the bevel of the cutting edge aligns with the blade of the try square.

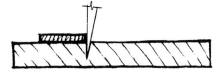

▲ *Angle blade* so that it aligns with try square blade.

◄ *Grip knife* with index finger on top of blade.

A proper knife mark is a clean, deep cut that shows very clearly when held to the light.

Try square

The try square guides the knife when squaring round the workpiece and checks the squareness of the workpiece once cut.

Grip The try square grip is common to many woodworking tools. Three fingers press against the far side of the workpiece, thumb presses against the stock, and index finger presses down on the blade.

Thumb presses the stock against the face edge or face side, three fingers press against the opposite edge or side and index finger pressed down on the blade. It's also possible to reverse the position of thumb and three fingers.

PRACTICE   *Square the end 1*
marking knife and try square

Begin by incising a line around the end. Knife the face side first. Register the stock of the square against the face edge and lay the blade across the face side. Aim to remove as little wood as possible, but if you get less than 1/16 in. (1.5mm) from the end, the knife tends to shave off a slice of wood instead of incising a line.

▲ *Try square* grip – stock against face edge, blade across face side.

▲ *Same procedure,* grip reversed.

Before making the second cut, rotate the wood through 90°. It doesn't matter whether you knife the face edge next or the opposite edge. It *does* matter that you reference the stock of the try square against the face side to make the next incision.

Locate the outside edge of the try square blade about an inch inside the line just incised. Insert the knife into the line where it exits from the corner of the workpiece. Make sure knife face is vertical. Then slide the try square up to it.

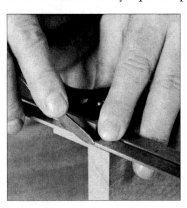

▲ *Seat knife* in the corner cut, then slide square to the knife.

▶ *Incise line* across edge. Hold stock against face side.

Using the knife to position the try square is simpler and more accurate than trying to move the try square into the exact spot, guided by nothing more than eyesight. To ensure the knife lines meet exactly at the fourth corner, the try square stock goes against the face side or face edge for every mark made.

PRACTICE   *Square the end 2*
smoothing plane

To plane end grain you need a heavy plane fitted with a sharp blade. For a 5 in. (125mm) end the best choice is an 04 or 04½ smoothing plane. Its sole is plenty long for the job and it has enough heft for smooth, effective planing. A block plane is the wrong tool – it's too light.

Be sure the knife line on the far edge of the wood is deep enough to prevent the fibers from splitting out. As you approach the knife line shaving by shaving, the tissue will crumble away to the depth of the incision. This tells you exactly where the actual planed surface is in relation to the intended finished surface.

◄ *Grip and arm position for planing end grain. Extend index finger along the frog for better control.*

The closer you get to the knife line, the more apparent the accuracy of your approach becomes. The knife line will show as a shiny or lighter mark around the workpiece, indicating where partial shavings need to be removed

If you must remove the ghost of a shaving from the far end of the wood and you're worried this final pass will cause a split, turn the wood around in the vise. What was the far edge of the cut is now the near edge. Make a tapered shaving by lifting the plane off the wood about half way across.

Checking for square Hold the square by the stock and register it against the face edge. Press the stock in the center to ensure good contact.

Hold the inside edge of the blade about an inch above the workpiece and then lower it onto the end. Check several locations, back to front. Lift the try square and reposition for each check. – don't slide the blade across the workpiece.

◄ *Check planing accuracy with a try square.*

Because light amplifies the smallest inaccuracy, hold the workpiece toward a light. The try square shows whether or not the end of the wood is square, but if it's not square, the tool doesn't measure how far it's off. You must judge the degree and location of error from the amount of light squeezing through the space between wood and tool.

Gauge the shoulder line

Hand woodworkers use three gauges. All are held and operated the same way. Learn to use the cutting gauge well and you will know how to use the other two.

Cutting gauge

The gauge is pushed, not pulled, to make the knife line. Control and a light grip rather than strength are the keys to skillful use.

◄ *Grip the gauge with the thumb on the back edge of the fence.*

▲ *Set the gauge to about 1/32 in. (.75mm) less than the thickness of the wood.*

Grip Assuming that you are right handed, hold the gauge in your right hand with your index finger wrapped round the edge of the fence. Place your remaining three fingers round the stock. Place your thumb on the back edge of the fence, positioned so that it drives the knife forward.

PRACTICE **Gauge the face**
cutting gauge

Hold the gauge and workpiece as shown in the photo. Hold the board in your left hand, one edge down on the bench, the board at an angle of about 70° and overhanging the end to allow the gauge to pass unimpeded across its face. (On a very wide board, say 24 in. (600mm) or more, the workpiece is usually held flat on the bench; it's easier to handle that way and won't slide about.) Apply pressure in two directions at once: inward against the end of the workpiece and downward across its face. The inward pressure is applied mainly by the inside face of the second finger pressing hard against the fence.

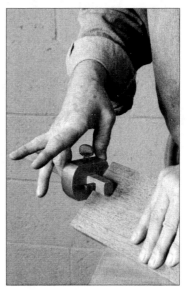

▲ **Apply pressure** in two directions at once: inward and downward.

▶ **Inward pressure** is applied mainly by the second finger of the gauge hand.

PRACTICE *Gauge the edge*
cutting gauge

Gauge the edge of the board by placing the it flat on the bench, as shown below. Gauge the far edge with a downward stroke. Concentrate on the contact between fence and workpiece, but relax your grip on the tool – you only have a short line to cut.

Control is much more important than force. If either wood or gauge gets out control, chances are you are applying too much force in the wrong direction.

◀ *Gauge far edge* with a downward stroke, board flat on the bench.

▲ *View* of face and edge gauge lines.

Mark the tail cuts

Use the sliding bevel to mark out the sloping tail part of a dovetail joint. You mark joint guidelines on one side of the board only, the side facing you when you saw. Now comes the decision, Which side to mark – face side or outside? One concern is tearout from the saw. On some woods with some saws you may get some tearout. With a dovetail saw it's on the back, with a dozuki it's on the front. It's a minor nuisance that usually disappears once the joint is glued and certainly disappears after you've cleaned up the surface which projects beyond the end grain. I always mark and cut from the outside, that is, face side at the back. Working this way, you see and saw the joint line which is visible when the job is finished. Any deviation from the joint line on the face side is hidden inside the joint.

Sliding bevel

Set the sliding bevel to the desired slope by drawing the slope on a board or the bench top. To plot a slope of 1:5, for example, mark a line AB with a try square at right angles to the bench edge and 5 in. (125mm) long. Locate point C on the bench edge 1 in. (25mm) from point A. The line BC forms a I:5 slope. Set the sliding bevel by simply putting the stock of the tool against the edge of the bench and aligning the blade with the sloping line.

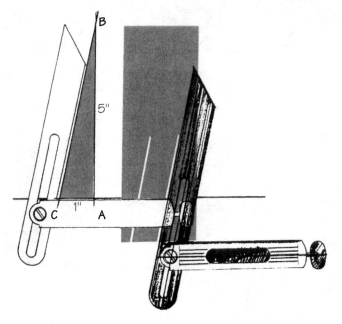

◀ *Use a board or the bench top to plot your preferred dovetail slope. This one is 1:5.*

Lay out the tail practice as in the drawing below. First, square across the end grain, then mark the slopes. Turn the sliding bevel left or right to keep as much of the stock on the end grain as possible.

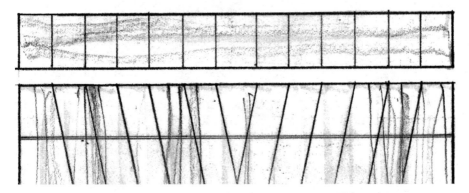

▲ Mark the lines at 3/8 in. (10mm) intervals. Draw half one way and half the other way.

▲ **Measure layout** with a rule. Clamp practice wood in the vise so the end grain is high enough for easy marking.

▲ **Square the intervals** across the end grain with a sharp B pencil.

◀ ▲ **Mark a slope** from each interval with sliding bevel. Extend the line down the wood about 2 in. (50mm).

Make the tail cuts

Sawing is the heart of the matter. I've broken it down into a sequence of steps, beginning with how to hold the saw and where to stand when making the cut.

Grip   Grip the saw firmly with your index finger extended as shown, but not white-knuckle tight. The triangulation between index finger and little finger provides steering control.

▲ **Grip** saw firmly, thumb over the middle finger.

▲ **Extend** index finger forward and resting on the handle.

Stance   Establish foot position by working back from the correct saw position. The saw must move back and forth at right angles to the workpiece, much like a piston. The saw can only move this way if your wrist, lower arm, upper arm, and shoulder joint form a straight line.

Place one foot in front of the other, as if you were taking a long walking step, crouch slightly, and bend forward to see the work clearly. Right-handers step the left foot forward, lefties step right foot forward.

If your wrist is cocked out of line, it's because you are standing too far left or right of the intended saw cut. Reposition your feet to get the piston-like alignment described above. Misalignment of wrist, arm, and shoulder is the major cause of the saw jamming in the kerf and wandering from the guideline. Moving your feet an inch or two left or right is usually the only correction required.

Rest your other hand lightly on the workpiece. Guide the saw with the edge of your thumb to start the cut.

▲ **Place** your left hand lightly on the workpiece. Saw, wrist, lower arm, upper arm and shoulder joint form a straight line.

▲ **The longer** the step, the deeper the crouch and the closer your eyes are to the work. Distribute your weight evenly on both feet.

Place the workpiece vertically in the vise so that it projects 2 in. (50mm) above the jaws. You now have to saw at an angle to the vertical.

You could angle the workpiece in the vise so that the the saw cut is vertical, but this entails a lot of fuss and bother. First, you must check with a try square to make sure the guidelines are truly vertical. Second, you must angle the workpiece in the opposite direction – and check again for vertical with a try square – when making the second series of cuts. Third, and worst of all, you must start the cut on a sloping surface.

Rather than struggle with all these variables, choose a constant that is quick and easy to achieve: clamp the workpiece vertically in the vise. Then learn to saw at an angle – it's not that difficult.

▲ ▶ **Place workpiece** *tight against the vise support bar and aligned with a vertical reference line knifed into the rear vise jaw. Clamp workpiece about 2 in. (50mm) above the jaws.*

A tail cut has two characteristics:

- it's at right angles to the tail piece
- it's a straight line

Sawing is a two step procedure. In Step 1, you establish a guide kerf at right angles to the face of the workpiece. In Step 2, you angle the saw to follow the sloped pencil guideline. With practice, you can combine Steps 1 and 2 in a single fluid action, sawing continuously with long, even strokes.

PRACTICE   *Tail cuts*
dovetail saw

Start by sawing down the outside of the line nearest an edge. Begin the cut on the far side of the end grain. Hold the saw vertical in front elevation with the tooth edge slightly raised at the heel in side elevation. Start with a pull stroke, using 90 per cent of the saw blade. Don't apply downward pressure, simply use the weight of the saw. Make the guide kerf no deeper than the length of the saw teeth and make the bottom of the kerf horizontal. Once the guide kerf has been cut, tilt the saw right or left to follow the pencil guide-line down to the shoulder line.

▼ **Start cut** with a light touch on the far side of the workpiece, saw raised slightly at the heel. Rest your left hand on the workpiece to guide the saw with your thumb to begin the cut.

▼ **Holding** the saw at right angles, cut the guide kerf to the depth of the teeth. The pencil line is your guide.

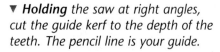

◄ ▲ **With the guide kerf** established, tilt the saw and follow the line. Set the angle by looking at the pencil guideline marked on the workpiece.

▲ **Practice tail cuts.** The first four cuts descend to the shoulder line. The fifth cut is a guide kerf.

▲ **Check** your work for square. Make sure the cut doesn't extend beyond the shoulder line on either side.

Once you begin the downward cut, keep the kerf straight. It doesn't matter if the saw wanders a little off the angle of the guide line, but the cut face must be a flat plane regardless of the angle. A curved cut is useless because you cannot fit it accurately to the mating part of the joint. This will become clearer when you make a complete dovetail joint.

1 *Make the guide kerf square across the end grain, holding the saw vertical.*

2 *Once the guide kerf is established, tilt the saw and cut down the guideline.*

3 *Don't adjust the saw part way down the cut. Once committed to a slope, stick with it.*

No handsaw removes its own waste efficiently. When sawdust builds up in the kerf, it becomes trapped and pushes the blade off course. At the first sign of wandering, remove the saw from the cut and blow out the sawdust.

If you learn how to saw down the workpiece with the tooth edge horizontal, you won't have to keep checking the stop point on the back side of the workpiece: you will know how close the saw cut is to the shoulder line. Be bold and go for it. Once you have made a few correct cuts confidence will follow.

The following points are common to all handsaws:

- Align saw and arm so that they move in the same plane, like a piston.

- Stand in a comfortable, balanced, crouched position.

- Start the cut by raising the heel of the saw slightly.

- Start the cut using only the weight of the saw as the downward force.

- Don't force the saw by sawing too quickly. Use long even strokes – let the tool do the job.

- If the saw strays from the line, stop sawing and blow sawdust from the kerf.

Mark the pin cuts

Once you are satisfied with the accuracy of your tail cuts, prepare to make some pin cuts by squaring the ends of your now shrinking practice wood.

When making a complete dovetail joint, you mark the pins from the tails. However, since you are still at the practice stage and lack a finished set of tails, you'll mark the pins using a sliding bevel set at the same 1:5 slope used earlier for making the tails. On the real joint this mark is made with a knife – use one for this practice.

Lay out the pin cuts as in the drawing below.

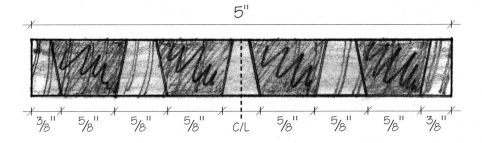

▲ **Mark layout** with rule, with workpiece upright in the vise.

▲ **Mark end grain** lines with marking knife and sliding bevel.

◀ **Mark cutting guideline** 2–3 in. (50–75mm) long with sharp B pencil and try square.

Make the pin cuts

A pin cut has two characteristics:

- it splits the knife line

- it's vertical to the end grain

Sawing pins is a two-step procedure. In Step 1 you establish the guide kerf across the end grain by splitting the knife line. In Step 2 you saw straight down the face of the workpiece, guided by the pencil line.

Learning to cut the kerf tight to the knife line is worth all the practice you can stand because the joint is made right or wrong in the few seconds and five or six saw strokes it takes you to do Step 1. The tails may be perfect, your pin cuts may be perfectly vertical, but if you're not right on the knife line every time, then the joint cannot be a perfect fit.

PRACTICE   *Pin cuts*
            dovetail saw

Clamp the workpiece vertically in the vise. Begin the pin cut as you did the tail cut, and keep the saw blade vertical in front elevation. Concentrate on making the guide kerf follow the knife line across the wood. Aim to get the teeth horizontal by the time the guide kerf is as deep as the length of the teeth. Remove one half of the V of the knife line, leaving the other half all the way across the wood.

To better see how closely the kerf follows the knife line, inspect the work through a hand lens.

 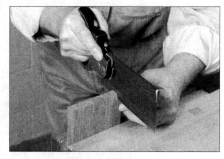

Split the knife line as you come across the end grain. You establish the guide kerf in about half a dozen strokes.

With the guide kerf established, saw straight down the wood. The pencil guide line tells you where vertical lies.

Remove bulk waste

Removing the bulk of the waste in the sockets and cleaning up the shoulder lines is the same for tails and pins. However, I have left these operations until now because tail sockets, being bigger than pin sockets, make for easier practice.

To remove the bulk of the waste, you have two choices:

- saw it out with a coping saw
- chop it out with a chisel and mallet

My preference, by a long shot, is to saw. It's quick, it's clean, and by sawing carefully and close to the line, you reduce the time and effort of chiseling flat to the knife line.

Sawing out the waste

Using the coping saw is very different from using other Western handsaws. First, you have two hands on the handle; second, it saws on the pull stroke; third, you stand with your feet apart but parallel to the bench – not in the walking stance of the backsaw.

If you encounter difficulties, the most likely causes are using the coping saw like a backsaw in grip and stance, and sawing too quickly.

Grip   Hold the saw in your right hand, thumb on top of and in line with the handle, fingers curled round in a comfortable grip for pulling the tool. Enclose the right hand in your left hand, thumb sitting on top of the handle.

◄ *Coping saw grip.*

Mount the workpiece in vise with the shoulder line projecting about three inches.

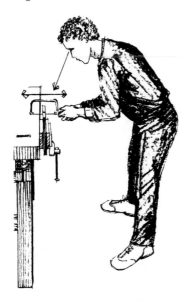

Stance Stand facing the workpiece in the vise, feet slightly more than shoulder-width apart in a line parallel to the workpiece, and body bent to make room for the reciprocal arm movement and to bring your eyes close to the sawcut.

Position the blade in the saw so that the teeth are pointing down: the blade holding pins are vertical and in line with the frame. If you insert the blade of the coping saw into the dovetail saw kerf so that it is moving forward and downward at the same time, the kerf walls will not be damaged by the saw teeth. It's usually easier for right-handed workers to put the saw in the right hand kerf and saw toward the left hand kerf.

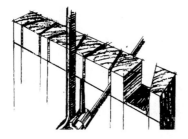

◄ *To avoid damaging the kerf walls, insert the blade into the dovetail kerf while moving it simultaneously forward and downward.*

Motion   The key to sawing a tight curve or turning the saw at right angles is to keep the saw moving the full extent of its stroke while gently turning the blade so that its teeth enlarge the kerf by rubbing away the wood from the kerf walls. Don't try to turn the blade without sawing. If you do, the blade will jam and likely break.

Use all the blade, and move the saw by flexing the arm muscles at the elbows and shoulders to it move back and forth like a piston. At this point the key is moving the saw slowly back and forth. Focus more on the correct motion than the correct cut.

The orientation of the blade in two planes is critical, but because the blade is so thin, the tendency is to succeed in one plane but fail the other. When the workpiece is vertical in the vise, the blade should be horizontal in side elevation and at right angles to the workpiece in plan. With practice you can check the orientation as you work, but as a beginner you may have to stop sawing to make the check.

PRACTICE   *Removing waste*
coping saw

The better the cut you make with the coping saw, the less work you will have to do with the chisel. You have to tilt the saw to remove the waste on the pin piece and you should work with the face side away from you so as not to mar the outside shoulder.

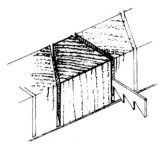

▲ **Drop the blade** to the bottom of the kerf , then lift it about 1/16 in. (1.5mm). This is the amount of waste wood that will be left above the knife line. Keep the blade horizontal at all times.

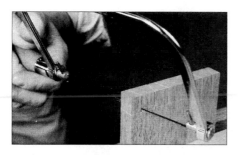

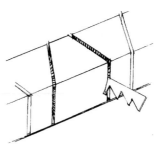

▲ **Tilt the the saw frame** about 15° until there is moderate resistance from the twisted blade. Use the resistance to steady the blade in the kerf. Now begin to saw at a slow and steady pace, using all the blade. As the teeth widen the kerf, continue to tilt the frame, keeping slight tension on the blade.

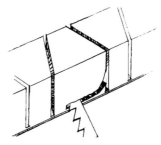

▲ **Concentrate** on the turning action: the aim is to turn the blade in its own width. Once the frame is horizontal, continue the cut across the wood.

▲ ▶ **Your pace** is smooth and unhurried, but because the coping saw is so efficient, the waste pieces are removed rapidly and effortlessly.

Dozuki workaround The saw kerf made by a dozuki saw is too narrow to accept a coping saw blade. To solve the problem, saw down the waste beside the kerf with the coping saw and remove a section that will then allow you to turn the blade and saw across the grain to remove the remainder of the waste. Because the coping saw cuts quickly, the extra cut takes hardly any time.

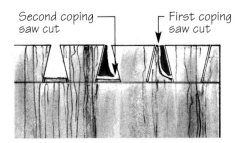

◀ *Make an extra cut with the coping saw to remove waste between narrow kerf dozuki saw cuts.*

Beware chopping out the waste

Chopping out the waste is a risky operation. Chances are high you will create a cavity right under the knife line. I'll discuss the operation briefly to clarify why you should avoid it.

Working on a cutting board, hold the chisel vertical about 1/4 in. (6mm) from the knife line and strike it with a mallet. Now flip the board and chop from the other side. After several more strikes the waste will come free, but instead of two chisel cuts meeting cleanly in the middle as you might expect, the wood instead collapses and a chunk is torn out under the knife line. Trying to chisel to the knife line by either vertical or horizontal paring only enlarges the cavity because it continues to collapse upon itself.

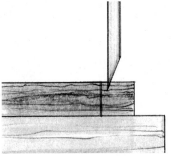

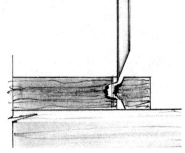

▲ *First side, single chop 1/4 in. (6mm) from knife line – no problem so far.*

▲ *Second side, final chops – the waste collapses under the knife line.*

Clean up the shoulders

The shoulders of the dovetail joint are made clean and square with a chisel. Cutting with a chisel is called paring. There are two types of paring:

- vertical paring

- horizontal paring

There's a separate technique for each type and you'll use both when making a dovetail joint.

The word vertical is used loosely. To pare consistently vertical is hardly possible, so it's futile to try. If you do try, you will likely undercut the shoulder on the opposite side. Instead, hold the chisel 5° to 10° less than vertical and adopt the following method.

Put the workpiece on a cutting board to protect the bench. Begin by establishing the shoulder on one side by "vertical" paring. Next flip the workpiece and establish the other shoulder in the same way. The result is a mound of wood in the center, with very accurate and visible shoulder lines on each side.

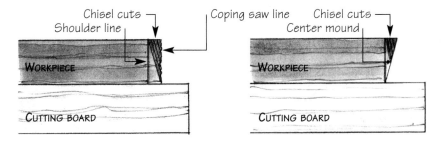

▲ *Stage 1 cuts – establish the shoulder line with several cuts. Angle the chisel 5-10° to avoid undercutting the shoulder on the opposite side.*

▲ *Stage 2 cuts– flip the board, angle the chisel, and make several cuts, leaving a center mound of wood between the shoulder lines.*

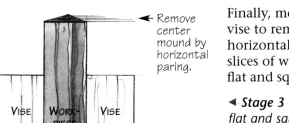

Finally, mount the workpiece in the vise to remove the center mount by horizontal paring. Remove thin slices of wood to make the shoulder flat and square.

◄ *Stage 3 cuts– make the shoulder flat and square to the face side by horizontal paring.*

In both paring methods one hand powers the chisel while the other hand guides it. The second hand also acts at times as a brake and occasionally supplies extra power. If you're right-handed, your right hand is the power hand. From here on I'll distinguish one from the other with the names power hand and guide hand.

Vertical paring

Grip   Grip the chisel like a dagger with your power hand, thumb over the end. Bend your arm so the chisel sticks out horizontally from your shoulder, then bend at the waist until you're looking down at the workpiece. The chisel should now be vertical.

Stance   Cut downward by bending your body from the hip and knees. There is no independent arm movement. Lock your upper body so that the back of your hand and the back of your head moves down as far as the chisel edge. Rest the back of the guide hand firmly on the workpiece, with the chisel between the thumb and index finger.

Making small slices at a slight angle, work methodically back to the knife line. Make the final cut when you feel the chisel "lock into" the knife line. Turn the workpiece over and repeat the procedure from the other side. Vertical paring leaves a cut that starts in the knife line on each face. The next step is to remove the central mound by horizontal paring.

◀ *Vertical paring –Grip the chisel like a dagger with the power hand. Support the chisel between thumb and index finger with the guide hand.*

Apply force by bending your body from the hip.

Horizontal paring

Grip   Grip the chisel in your power hand as though it were as extension of your forearm. Set the handle end in the cup of your palm, with the thumb on the top of the handle and the index finger down the side. Clamp the workpiece vertically in the vise.

◄ ▲ *Grip. Lay the back of the guide hand on the cheek of the vise and against the workpiece. Rest the chisel on the index finger of the left hand. Position the thumb atop the chisel to control cutting action.*

Stance   Step back with your right foot and lock your arms against your chest and hips.

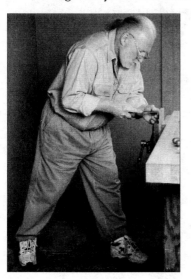

◄ *Stance. Make the cut by pushing from the legs and back. Keep your arms locked against your body.*

There is very little wood to remove in total, but by cutting thin shavings, you will gradually make a flat cut across the end grain.

Confirm that the bottom of the tail and pin sockets are flat by checking with a square from both sides.

If the square touches the visible shoulder when checked from both sides, the surface between the shoulders may be flat, which is good. It may also be hollow, which is bad. Avoid undercutting socket bottoms for two reasons: first, when you clamp the joint you will crush the edges of the dished portion and change the inside dimension; second, if you are over-zealous when cleaning up the faces of the workpiece, the more surface tissue you remove, the more visible becomes the joint line.

◀ *Confirm that the bottom of the tail socket is flat by checking from both sides with a try square.*

Using muscle power on hardwoods such as oak and maple makes for difficult and tiring work. A mallet will make the work easier. Follow the same technique as for vertical paring, working from first one side then the other to remove the center mound. Put down the mallet and finish the job by horizontal paring powered by muscle.

◀ *Use a mallet if the wood is too hard to pare by hand.*

Vertical paring sequence for cleaning up the shoulders of the tail sockets

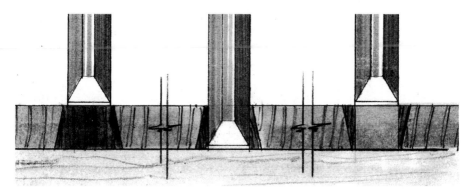

1 *Put the wide side of the socket down on a cutting board. Face side of the workpiece is up. Choose a chisel as wide as the narrow side of the socket.*

2 *Pare down at an angle, leaving a wedge of uncut material at either side of the socket.*

3 *Flip workpiece and pare down, following the chisel track already established. Leave a mound in the center and the wedges at either side for removal by vertical and horizontal paring.*

▲ **Follow chisel track** *established by vertical paring from the narrow side of the socket.*

▲ **Remove** *central mound and wedges by horizontal paring.*

Making a stopped socket

Mark out a joint

Only on a through dovetail do both tail piece and pin piece have open sockets. On the single lap, double lap, and secret miter joints, one or both pieces have stopped sockets. Prepare for the practice by cutting the ends of your board square. If you have already repeated several of the previous practice cuts, you may need a new board. Mark the dimensions as shown.

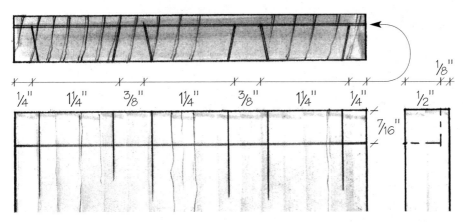

¹⁄₄"   1¹⁄₄"   ³⁄₈"   1¹⁄₄"   ³⁄₈"   1¹⁄₄"   ¹⁄₄"   ¹⁄₂"

¹⁄₈"

⁷⁄₁₆"

This practice simulates making the pin piece of a single lap on a drawer front. Normally, the tail piece, which is the drawer side, is made first as though it were part of a through joint. Then the pin piece, which is the drawer front, is marked from the tail piece. Since there is no tail piece for this practice, mark the pins using a marking knife, sliding bevel and B pencil.

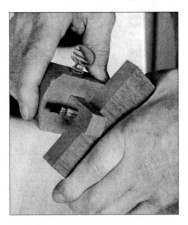

◄ *Make both marks* with a cutting gauge.

Gauge the end wall line from the face side with the gauge set to 1/2 in. (12.5mm).

Saw the sides

Sawing pins for a lap joint is very different from a through joint. With a through joint you begin the cut by placing the saw on the far corner, then bring the kerf toward you across the end grain. Not so with a lap joint. In this case you begin the cut on the near corner and extend the kerf away from you splitting the end grain knife line. The sawing sequence is divided into two stages. First, you establish the rim of the tail socket. Second, you saw down the vertical, following the pencil guideline.

Clamp the workpiece vertically in the vise, projecting about two inches, face side toward you.

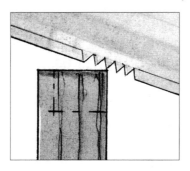

▲ *Stage 1* Raise the toe of the saw slightly and begin the cut on the near corner. Split the line.

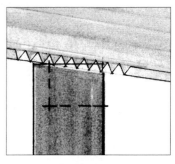

▲ Extend the guide kerf away from you toward the end wall gauge line. Make kerf no deeper than 1/16 in. (1.5mm).

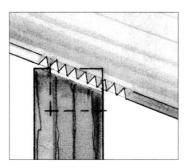

▲ *Stage 2* Extend the cut down toward the face side gauge line. Keep the saw in the kerf – don't tilt it out, but especially don't saw beyond the end wall gauge line.

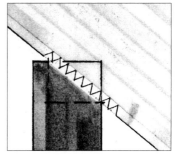

▲ You can saw only half the face. The remaining waste has to be removed with a chisel, using the sawn face as a guide.

▼ *Start cut* on near corner, then extend the guide kerf toward the end wall gauge line.

▼ *Extend cut* down to the face side gauge line, following the pencil guideline and keeping the saw fully in the kerf.

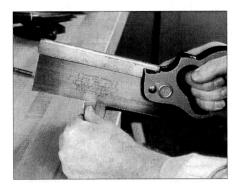

◀ *Stance* – Bend at the waist and knees to get a clear view of how you are cutting.

Chisel out the waste

Chisel out the waste in three stages:

- Stage 1– chop out the bulk waste

- Stage 2 – refine cuts to the shoulder lines

- Stage 3 – chisel the sawn face to the end wall

Stage 1 is one of the few woodworking tasks best done sitting down. Less stress on your limbs results in more accurate work at the bench. I use a saw horse as a seat.

Because this is not a through cut, no cutting board is required. Place the workpiece flat on the bench. Hold the mallet in one hand. Use the other hand to hold the chisel upright and in the correct spot, and to press the workpiece firmly in place on the bench.

Use the widest chisel that will fit the socket. Put it halfway between the face side gauge line and and the end of the workpiece. Drive the chisel to half the finished depth. Repeat for the entire row of sockets, one after the other.

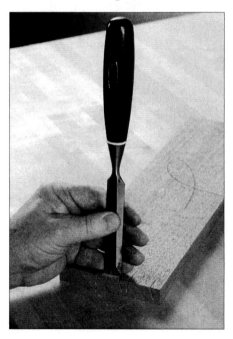

▲ *Grip* for holding the chisel.

▲ *Sit down* to chop out the bulk waste from a stopped socket.

Stage 1: chop out the bulk waste

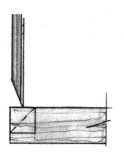
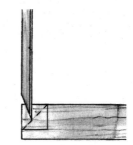

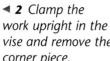

▶ *1 Drive chisel to half the finished depth.*

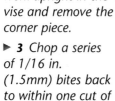

◀ *2 Clamp the work upright in the vise and remove the corner piece.*

▶ *3 Chop a series of 1/16 in. (1.5mm) bites back to within one cut of the face side gauge line.*

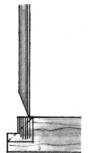
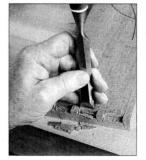

◀ *4 Chop a series of 1/16 in. (1.5mm) bites back to within one cut of the end grain gauge line.*

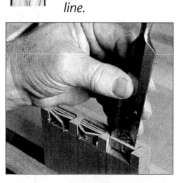

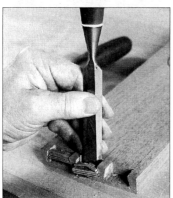

▲ *5 Free any remaining leaves of wood by chiseling across the end grain.*

Stage 2: refine cuts to the shoulder lines

▲ **1** *Clean back to the face side gauge line.*

▲ **2** *Pare the face of the end wall, face side away from you.*

◀ **3** *Check for parallel with blade of 6 in. (150mm) try square.*

▲ ▼ **4** *In preparation for Stage 3, cut across the end grain at the bottom of each socket below the sawn face using two 1/4 in. (6mm) skew chisels.*

▲ **5** *Check for square with try square.*

Stage 3: chisel the sawn face to the end wall

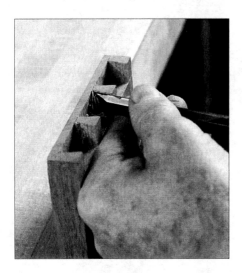

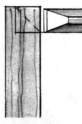

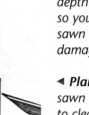

◀ *Side elevation –
The chisel should be
narrower than the
depth of the socket
so you can see the
sawn face. Don't
damage the rim.*

◀ *Plan – Use the
sawn face as a guide
to clean out the
waste.*

▲ *1 Clean up the pin faces.*

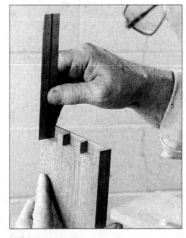

▲ *2 Complete clean up of the
corners.*

▲ *3 Check end wall is square
to shoulder.*

◀ *Finally…time to admire
your work.*

CHAPTER 4

Making a through dovetail

Of the four major dovetail types, the through dovetail is the most straightforward to make. (Refer to Chapter 1, *Through dovetail*, page 12.) For practice, prepare two workpieces 18 in. × 4 1/4 in. × 5/8 in. (450mm × 106mm × 16 mm). One is the tail piece, the other is the pin piece. Square the ends and mark the face sides and face edges. Make the joint with the face sides inside and the face edges at the same edge.

Marking out

The suggested layout shown below is not particularly elegant, but large pin sockets are easier to chisel flat than smaller ones. As you try different layouts, consider that the smaller the pin, the smaller the chisel needed to clean out the socket. Once the socket is less than 1/4 in. (6mm) wide, you must grind a chisel narrower or use a 1/8 in. (3mm) chisel, which may not be easily available. Also, very narrow chisels are more difficult to control because the area of the flat back which helps guide the chisel is so small.

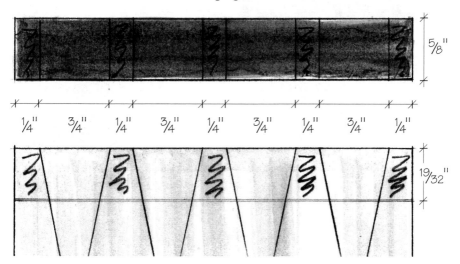

▲ **Through dovetail layout** for practice tail piece. Slope is 1:5. The wavy line marks the pin sockets – the material to be removed.

Note that the tail piece shoulder line is located from the end 1/32 in. (.75mm) less than the thickness of the 5/8 in. (16mm) pin piece.

Lay out and mark the tails

Begin by setting the cutting gauge to just less than the thickness of the wood. The captions say 1/32 in.(.75mm), but this is meant as guidance. With practice, you will learn to set the gauge by eye rather than a precise measurement.

▼ *Set a cutting gauge to 1/32 in. (.75mm) less then the thickness of the pin piece and square around the end.*

▼ *Lay out the end grain spacing with a sharp B pencil.*

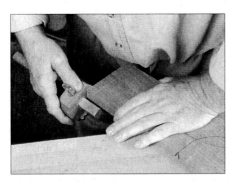

▲ *Square across the end grain marks with pencil and try square.*

▲ *Mark the tail slopes with pencil and sliding bevel. Set the sliding bevel to a 1:5 slope (or one you prefer) and extend the lines two or three inches past the gauge line.*

Saw the tails

Saw the tail slopes with the wood held upright in the vise. Then remove the bulk of the waste with a coping saw.

◀ ▼ *Saw the tail slopes. The kerf has two characteristics: it's at right angles to the tail piece and it's a straight line.*

◀ *Remove the bulk of the waste from the pin socket with a coping saw. The closer you saw to the line, the less chisel work you have to do.*

◀ *To saw off the outside half pin, clamp the workpiece horizontally in the vise. Make the cut about 1/16 in. (1.5mm) from the shoulder line.*

Clean up the shoulders

Clean up the shoulders by both vertical paring and horizontal paring, guided by the gauge knife lines.

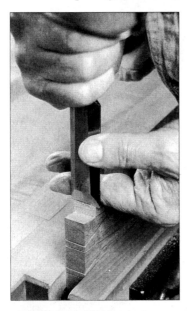

◄ *Square the edge shoulders* with a wide chisel. Position the chisel by looking at the flat back face and fitting it into the knife line.

▲ *Check for square* by pressing the chisel tight to the shoulder and measuring the angle at the back with a small try square.

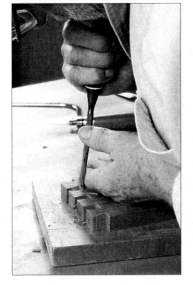

◄ *Establish the shoulder* at each side of the pin socket. Use a cutting board to protect the bench.

▲ *Slice off the center mound* in the socket by horizontal paring. Check the shoulders for flat with a try square.

Mark the pins from the tails

With the exception of the secret miter, all the major dovetail joints are made with the tails before the pins. Why this is so will become clear once you've finished marking out the pins.

◀ *Position the pin piece* upright in the vise so the end is projecting about 1/8 in. (3mm) and the face side is away from you.

Hold a block against the outside face of the pin piece so the block forms an aligned projection of the face. I use the stock of a 6 in. (150mm) try square with the blade removed.

▲ *Put the end* of the tail piece tight to the block, face side down.

▲ *Align edges* of pin piece and tail piece with a rule. If you disturb the end setting, reposition the block and reset the tail piece.

▶ *Hold setup firmly* by placing your fingers on the bench and lowering the heel and palm of your hand onto the tail piece.

Mark the pins from the tails (continued)

◀ ▼ *Mark the pins* from the tails using the point of your marking knife. Keep the blade of the knife flat and tight to the wall of the tails.

◀ *Reposition the workpiece* upright in the vise so it's projecting about 6 in. (150mm). With a sharp 2B pencil and try square, draw vertical guidelines from the end grain knife lines down the outside face.

You can now appreciate the logic of making the tails before the pins. If you make the pins first, you must devise a method of holding them in place while you mark out the tails. Imagine the awkwardness of holding the pin piece vertical and securely enough to accomplish the job. If you managed it, you now have to saw the tails. This time the kerf must have three characteristics: right angles to the pin piece, a straight line, plus spot on to the slope just marked. A tall order...and one best avoided.

Saw the pins and remove the waste

When you positioned the saw to cut the tails, it was of little consequence whether you positioned it left, right or center relative to the pencil guide line to make the kerf. Now, faced with a knife line to make the pins, you have no such flexibility. You have to split the line.

Once the shallow guide kerf is cut across the end grain, the pin is defined. It takes only a few strokes. You next saw straight down the grain, guided by the pencil line. The accuracy of your cut is evident once the two parts are brought together. Of course, the softer the wood, the more it will crush to accommodate pins cut too large – in this regard Honduras mahogany serves you well.

▼ ► *Split the line* with the initial saw cut, then saw straight down the workpiece using the pencil guidelines.

◄ *Remove the waste.* Avoid cutting into the pin by angling the coping saw blade to match the pin angle.

Clean up and check the shoulders

How to clean up and check the shoulders is described in Chapter 3, *Clean up the shoulders*, page 81.

Assemble the joint

Close the joint with a hammer. Tap each tail in turn. If the cuts are right, you will feel and hear the tail go into the socket. If the cuts are wrong, at some point you will be unable to drive the tail any further and the hammer sound will change to a sharper pitch. The need for touch and sound feedback is why you shouldn't assemble the joint with a mallet or use a protector pad. Don't worry, the hammer won't dent the wood.

▼ *Close the joint* with an 8- or 10-oz crosspeen hammer. The hammer face should be slightly domed and polished. Go across the work, tapping each tail in turn.

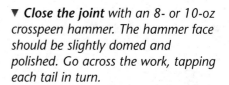

▼ *Enter the pins* by dropping the far end of the tail piece as you bring the joint together.

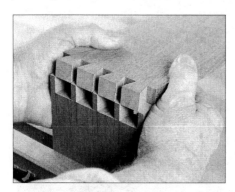

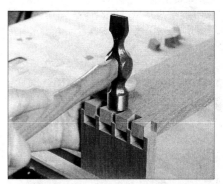

▲ *Pins and tails* fit snugly and the tail piece is slightly proud of the end grain pin piece.

▲ *To undo* the joint, protect the inside face with a scrap of wood as you tap it apart.

Glue the joint

The joint is not normally left in clamps while the glue dries. Close the joint by clamping each tail firmly in place and it will stay put, provided the joint is accurately made. If it won't stay put, make another joint, this time to a higher standard.

▼ *Use a flux brush* with the bristles cut short to apply glue to every face of both parts of the joint. Use the glue sparingly, but be sure to wet all mating surfaces.

▼ *Close the joint* as far as you can with a hammer.

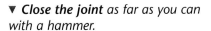

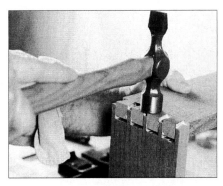

▲ *Clamp each tail.* Close 1, 2, and 3, then come back to 1. Close 4, then come back to 2. Close 5, then come back to 3. This clamping pattern prevents springback.

▲ *Clamp lightly* across the joint and use a protector pad.

The half pins have no dovetailing effect to keep them in place. In fact, the glue is trying to jack them away from the tail.

Mitered corner

Marking out a mitered corner using a Western miter square was always a crap shoot. You positioned the square by eye and hoped it was right – twice! My technique eliminates all the guesswork and gives a perfect result. It's used throughout this book.

To miter the corner of a through dovetail, mark out the tails as normal and make the joint, but ignore the outer two cuts. It might help to identify the outer lines with tape to remind yourself not to cut them.

All cuts except the outer edge cuts of the first and last tail are marked and made from the outside of the workpiece. The outer edge cuts are made from the *inside*, so be sure to mark these two slopes on the inside. To avoid making a mistake, it's best to not mark them on the outside when making the initial layout.

Mark the miter

▼ **Clamp the work** horizontal in the vise, projecting 3 to 4 in. (75–100mm). Working on the face side, put the point of your knife in the shoulder line about 1/8 in. (3mm) from the top edge. Hold the knife at right angles to the board.

◄ **Position** the Japanese miter square and slide it along the work until the mitered face of the bar meets the knife.

◄ **Hold** the miter square firmly in place and knife the miter shoulder line.

Saw the miter

Cutting the miter is similar to cutting any one of the stopped joints, a technique you practiced in Chapter 3.

◄ *Begin the cut* on the corner nearest you. Establish the kerf across the end grain then cut down the face, keeping the saw fully in the kerf.

◄ *Clamp* the workpiece high enough in the vise to allow you to end the cut with the saw angled at about 45°.

▲ ► *Turn the work* horizontal in the vise, then saw off the waste, laving the knife line intact. Saw gently and lift the saw before you cut into the face of the tail.

Pare the miter to the shoulder

Trim the miter by paring vertically with the work mounted horizontal in the vise.

◀ **Cut back** to the knife line by vertical paring with a chisel that is wider than the wood. Pare about 1/8 in. (3mm) away from the edge.

▲ **To prevent tearout** at the feather edge, leave a small blip of wood (indicated by the knife) until the end of the operation, then slice it off using the newly created flat as a guide.

◀ **Check** your work.

Mark pins from tails

To mark the miter, you have to knife inside an enclosed space. You may need to reshape the point of your knife to mark the far side.

◄ *Confirm the knife is tight to the tail face by bending down so you can see into the joint.*

Saw the pins

◄ ▼ *Mark the corner and cut the joint from this point on as for a through joint.*

◄ *Hold the two parts together to make sure which way the miter goes and determine which part must be cut.*

Mark and cut the miter

To knife the miter line, use exactly the same technique as described in the earlier section *Mark the miter*, page 102.

▼ *Saw off* the waste. Go slowly and gently at the end of the cut. I support the wood with a finger until the final stroke.

▼ *Pare back* to the miter line going down about 1/8 in. (3mm). Use a chisel wider than the cut, apply very light pressure, and leave the blip of wood at the feather edge.

◄ *Pare off* the waste wood horizontally with the wood held in the vise at about 45°. Use the newly created miter faces as your guide.

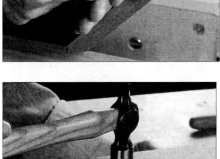

▲ ► *Close the joint* and celebrate.

Misfits

An over-large tail or pin can be made smaller to fit its socket. However, there's no rescue for a tail or pin made too small – you have to recut the joint. There are two types of misfit, and each has a specific rescue.

The first misfit occurs during assembly. The tail piece has been entered into the pin piece, but before it's fully home it becomes tight. The hammer bounces and the striking note changes. The tightness results from sawing the parts a little too rich. The face angles are fine, but you failed to cut tight enough to the line. The joint needs "easing." Removal of a very small amount of wood will ease the joint.

The second misfit is more extreme. The tails simply won't enter the tail sockets without damaging the inside edges of the tails or the end of the pins. We don't have a printable woodworking term for this condition. The rescue is called remodeling.

Easing the joint

Start by determining exactly where you must remove wood. Paring surfaces at random will only make matters worse. Two clues point you in the right direction. First, the hammer bounces and sounds a different note when it hits the tight tail. Second, the faces of a too-tight joint are glazed where the tissue has been compressed.

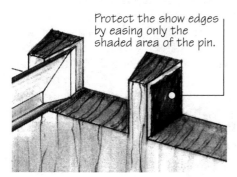

Protect the show edges by easing only the shaded area of the pin.

Once you've isolated the problem tail or tails, separate the joint and inspect the evidence. It's easier to adjust pins than tails because the large tail sockets give you more room to work in and the glazed, compressed area is easier to see. Remove a small slice of wood from the center portion of the face of the tight pin, but leave the outer or show edges of the joint intact. Chisel across the grain. Use a chisel narrower than the length of the face. On tail or pins 5/8 in. (16mm) long, use a 1/2 in. (12mm) chisel. Pare to within 1/16 in. (1.5mm) of the show edges, but go right across the back edge. If you have to ease more than one pin, do so.

Paring across the grain is preferable to paring down because you have greater control over how much wood you remove.

If you pare down the grain, you will, in theory, be safe half the time, that is, the grain will be in your favor and won't undercut. Other times the chisel will follow the grain and undercut the face.

Remodeling

If the tail cuts are straight and at right angles to the tail piece, then you've made a perfect set of tails. Since the pins are marked from the tails, the problem must lie in the pin piece. Inspect the end grain of the pin piece and you will find one or more places where you failed to saw close enough to split the line. A hand lens is a big help here. Putting it right takes a bold step. Mount the work vertically in the vise. Place the edge of a wide chisel in the knife line and re-establish it with slight vertical pressure or a slight tap with a mallet. *Don't cut down the face.* Next, square down the outer face of the pin with a marking knife, starting from the re-established end grain knife line. Square down the inside face the same way. You have now re-established all the outer edges of the pin. Now pare across the grain with a chisel as wide as the pin is long. Insert the chisel first in one face knife line then the other and make a clean cut that meets in the middle, guided by the end grain knife line.

Tail troubles

The tails should be accurate before you mark the pins from them. Two things can go wrong. The tail cut isn't straight, or it isn't at right angles to the tail piece. Both errors can best be avoided with more sawing practice. Easing the face of a tail is much the same as easing the face of a pin except you have less room in which to work. Pare across the grain, but don't cut through to the joint's show edges. To remodel the joint, establish where it's incorrectly cut, then mark around the problem area to re-establish the tail profile. Finally, pare across, first from side then the other, to meet in the middle of the tail face.

CHAPTER 5

Making a single lap dovetail

If you are making the joint as practice for a drawer front, you will likely work with two thicknesses of wood, one for the drawer front and the other for the drawer side. The drawer side is normally thinner than the drawer front. (Refer to Chapter 1, *Single lap dovetail*, page 14.) Prepare two pieces of wood, 18 in. × 4¼ in. × 11/16 in. (450mm × 106mm × 17.5mm) for the front piece and 18 in. × 4¼ in. × 1/2 in. (450mm × 106mm × 12.5mm) for the side piece.

Marking out

There are three lines to make using two gauge settings.

First setting, one line

The first setting determines the depth of the tail sockets. Set the gauge about 1/32 in. (.75mm) less than the thickness of the side piece.

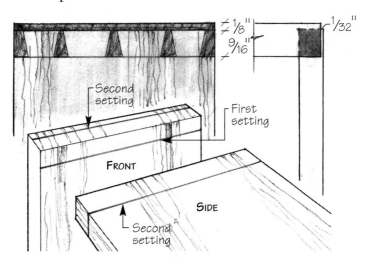

Second setting, two lines

The second setting determines the length of the tails, which is governed in part by how thick you want to make the end wall of the tail socket. No convention governs the wall thickness, but there are practical considerations.

Anything less than 1/8 in. (3mm) on a typical drawer slows down joint making because of the extra attention it demands: you can't afford to have the grain run backwards and make the end wall even thinner; you can't let your chisel go deeper into the wall tissue when cleaning up the end grain of the socket; and you have to be very careful not to overcut with the skew chisel. Since you are using 11/16 in. (17.5mm) material, set the gauge to 9/16 in. (14.5mm).

Note the gauge setting is not the wall thickness but rather the thickness of the front piece minus the desired wall thickness (11/16 - 1/8) (17.5mm - 3mm). The latter calculation also yields the length of the tails and this is the setting that is marked on both pieces of wood.

Mark the end wall from the face side of the front piece. Mark the tail length from the end grain of the side piece.

Gauge the three lines

▼ *First line* – *set the gauge to 1/32 in. (.75mm) less than the thickness of the side piece.*

▼ *Gauge the line across the face side of the front piece.*

▲ *Second & third lines* – *with the gauge set to leave the correct end wall thickness, gauge across the end of the front piece to mark the length of the tails.*

▲ *With the same gauge setting, mark round the side piece to knife the shoulder lines for the length of the tails.*

Lay out and mark out the tails

Lay out the tails on the side piece as for a through dovetail.

▲ **Mark out** the tail pin spacing on the end grain. With a sharp 2B pencil, square the lines across the end. Mark the slopes of the tails.

▲ **Check** that your narrow chisel will clean out the pin socket without crushing or cutting the tail tissue – very important if you like slim pins.

Saw the tails

Saw the tails as for a through dovetail.

◄ **Saw** the tail slopes. The kerf must be at right angles to tail piece and a straight line – on or off the slope a tad doesn't matter.

▲ **Remove** the bulk of the waste with a coping saw. The closer you saw to the line, the less chiseling required for cleanup.

Clean up the shoulders

Protect the bench with a cutting board.

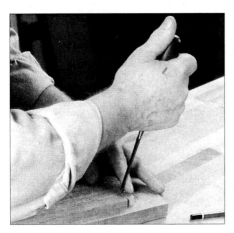

▲ ▶ *Establish the shoulder line* on *each side of the workpiece by vertical paring. To lock the chisel in the knife line, tilt the chisel forward so chisel edge and knife line are both visible.*

◀ *Square the shoulders* by horizontal *paring. Jack the workpiece up in the vise so you can work in a comfortable stance.*

Mark the pins from the tails

Positioning the tail piece on the pin piece may require several checks and adjustments.

◄ *Mount the pin piece* so that it projects about 1/8 in. (3mm) above the vise, face side inward. Set your marking knife in the gauge line on the end grain of the pin piece. Hold the knife vertical and slide the tail piece up to it. Repeat with knife in the opposite end of the gauge line.

▲ *Align the face edges* while aligning the tail piece with the gauge line of the pin piece.

► *Press tail piece* down firmly with the heel of your non-marking hand and mark the pins. Hold knife tightly aligned to the face of each tail.

▲ *Pins* marked out.

► *Mark vertical lines* from the end grain knife lines with a sharp 2B pencil.

Saw the pins

The operation is fully described in Chapter 3, *Making a stopped socket (Saw the sides)*, page 87.

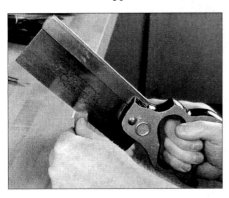

◄ **Start cut** on near corner, then extend it down to the face side gauge line.

Chop out the bulk waste

The operation is fully described in Chapter 3, *Chisel out the waste*, page 89.

▲ **Chop** a series of 1/6 in. (1.5mm) bites back to within one cut of the face side gauge line.

▲ **Chop** a series of 1/6 in. (1.5mm) bites back to within one cut of the end grain gauge line.

Refine cuts to the shoulder lines

Put the workpiece in the vise to pare back to the end wall of the socket. Make the final cut with the chisel locked into the gauge line on the end grain. Don't fret about the cleanup sequence – down the grain first, then across the grain, or vice versa? There is no practical advantage one over the other. You choose.

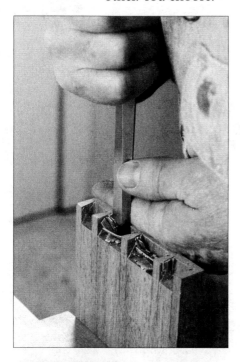

◄ *Take care* if the grain runs into the end wall. Cut back with very small slices, working from the bottom of the joint.

▼ *Sight for parallel* using a straight edge to project the outer surface. Hold the chisel in the socket to project the socket wall.

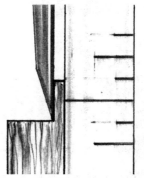

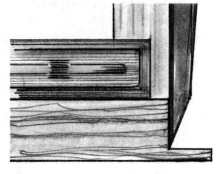

▲ *Clean back* to the shoulder line by vertical paring.

▲ *Sight for square* using the chisel to project the socket end grain.

Chisel the sawn face to the end wall

▼ *Clean up* the walls of the pins by first cutting the end grain of the waste. The skew chisel is shaped and sharpened specifically for this job.

▼ *Pare the shoulder* horizontally into the corner of the socket.

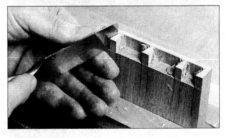

▲ *Cut the waste*, using the sawn portion of the pin as a guide. Use a chisel narrower than the length of the pin. Apply minimal force because you are making an easy cut across long grain.

▲ *Avoid paring* with a wide chisel because it hides the face to be cut. The slightest off-vertical shaving alters the rim of the pin.

CHAPTER 6

Making a double lap dovetail

Of the four major joints, the double lap is the most complicated to mark out because the each piece is marked differently. Only one piece has a rabbet. (Refer to Chapter 1, *Double lap dovetail*, page 16.)

Prepare two pieces of wood 18 in. × 4½ in. × 11/16 in. Note that both pieces must be the same thickness. Face sides are inside. Make all marks with the face of the cutting gauge on the face side or on the end grain.

Marking out

There are five lines to gauge, but only three gauge settings. The drawings show the tail piece horizontal and the pin piece vertical.

First gauge setting, three lines

1 Mark the pin socket end wall, which is also the rabbet wall line.

Set the cutting gauge to 9/16 in. from the face side and mark across the end grain of the tail piece and about 1/8 in. down the face edge and opposite edge.

2 Mark the tail socket end wall line

From the face side, mark across the end grain of the pin piece.

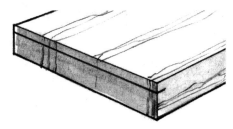
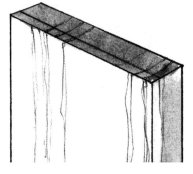

▲ *First line* – tail piece, view is face side down.
▶ *Second line* – pin piece, view is face side out

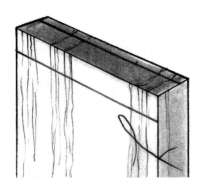

3 Mark the tail socket shoulder line.

From the end grain, mark across the face side of the pin piece. The tail socket shoulder line determines the length of the pins.

◄ *Third line – pin piece, viewed from the face side.*

Second gauge setting, one line

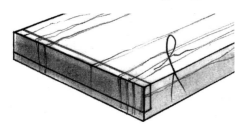

4 Mark the second line of the rabbet.

Set the gauge to 1/8 in. From the end grain, mark across the face side of the tail piece and across the edges to meet the first gauge line.

▲ *Fourth line – tail piece upside down, viewed from the face side.*

Third gauge setting, one line

5 Mark the pin socket shoulder line.

Set the gauge to the thickness of the wood. From the end grain, mark across the face side of the tail piece. The pin socket shoulder line determines the length of the tails.

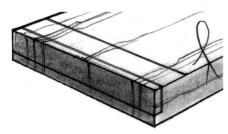

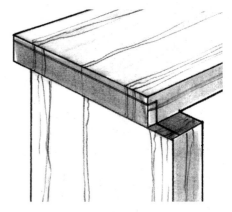

▲ *Fifth line – tail piece upside down, viewed from the face side.*
► *Correct marking out confirmed: All lines meet.*

Make the rabbet

You can make the rabbet by hand or machine. Either way the rabbet must be absolutely accurate. By hand, the tool of choice is a shoulder plane. By machine, choose a table-mounted router equipped with a spiral cutter and a solid straight fence.

◀ *A properly-tuned* shoulder plane makes quick work of a rabbet.

▲ **Check the rabbet**, hand-made or machine-made, with a try square.

▲ **Bring the parts** together to confirm that the contact faces are straight and at right angles.

Mark the tails

Chiseling the parts of the joint is easier if you make pins and tail approximately equal in size. The major consideration with the double lap and the secret miter joints is strength. You increase strength by increasing the number of glue lines. A suggested layout is shown below.

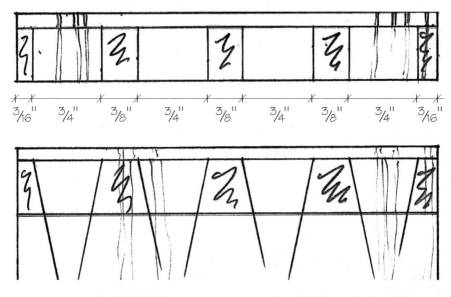

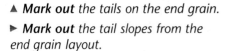

▲ **Mark out** the tails on the end grain.

▶ **Mark out** the tail slopes from the end grain layout.

Saw the tails

Because the wall of the rabbet is in the way, you can't first establish the right angle end grain cut then make the sloping tails cut as in other joints. Here the cuts have to proceed together. If you saw into the corner of the rabbet return, the error will show. You may wish to make some practice cuts first.

Set the saw stationary in the right plane for one line and focus your attention on the second line when starting the cut.

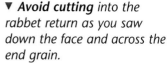

◀ *Alternate* *your attention between the end grain guideline and the face grain guideline during the cut.*

▼ *Avoid cutting* *into the rabbet return as you saw down the face and across the end grain.*

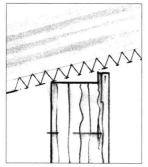
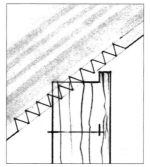
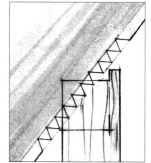

Clean out the bulk waste

Sit on a low chair or sawhorse so you see the work clearly and be comfortable as you do it. Place the workpiece on the bench – there's no need for a cutting board.

◄ *Cut across* the grain about half way down the joint. The corner portion usually comes free. Carry on cutting 1/16 in. slices, stopping within one cut of the shoulder.

◄ *Remove* the remaining bulk waste with the work upright in the vise. You cannot get very close to the end wall of the pin socket because of the restricted saw cut.

Clean back to the shoulders

◀ **Establish** the shoulder line at the base of the socket by horizontal paring.

▲ **Extend** the face of the tail established by the saw. Pare with a chisel that is narrower than the length of the tail so you can see where and how to hold the chisel. Taking small slices, cut back to the plane of the sawn face.

▲ **Cut the end grain shoulder** flat by vertical paring, using the gauged shoulder line as a reference.

▶ **Clean up** the end wall of the socket by vertical paring. Orient face side of workpiece toward bench.

Check all cuts for square and parallel with a try square.

Miter the tail piece corners

Put the workpiece horizontal in the vise and mark the corner miter as described in Chapter 4, *Mark the miter*.

▼ *Hold the point* of the knife in the shoulder line at right angles to the face side. Slide the Japanese miter square to the knife, hold the square firmly, and knife the line.

▼ *Remove most of the waste* by chisel. Clamp the work in the vise at about 45° and pare carefully to avoid slicing off the corner of the rabbet return.

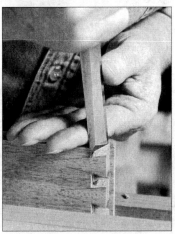

◄ *Establish the miter* by locking the chisel in the knife line and cutting about halfway across the miter.

Working this way, you will not undercut the corner of the rabbet as you pare the final couple of cuts and you can see both knife lines that are your guides.

Mark the pins from the tails

Because of the small enclosed space presented by the pin sockets, conventional marking knives are too large to mark the pins of a double lap dovetail. I re-shaped a Swiss Army knife to a point to do the job.

▲ *Mount the pin piece* in the vise so that it projects about 1/8 in. above the bench top. Position the tail piece. Align the edges. Hold firmly and mark the pins. Get down low to clearly see the location of the marking knife.

▲ *Extend the pin marks,* if necessary. Square down the face side with a sharp 2B pencil.

Saw the pins

The pin piece of a double lap joint resembles the pin piece of a single lap and it's made the same way. (See Chapter 4, *Saw the pins and remove the waste,* page 99). Begin by sawing a guide kerf across the end grain. Aim to be on the waste side and split the line.

Clean out the bulk waste

By now you will have developed your own order of moves to establish the shoulder lines by first chopping back with chisel and mallet followed by vertical and horizontal paring.

◄ *Avoid taking* too big a bite as you chop out the waste or you might bust out the end wall.

▲ ► *Clean back* to the shoulder lines in any order that suits you.

◄ *The skew chisel* chases the last splinters from the corners.

Miter the pin corner

The procedure is the same as mitering the pin corner on a through joint, with one exception – there is no feather edge.

▼ **Determine the position** of the miter line with knife and Japanese miter square, then knife the line.

▼ **Saw off the waste** as close as possible to the knife line.

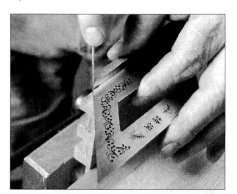

◄ **Establish the miter** face by vertical paring – keep off the very edge.

Complete the miter using the face you just cut as a guide. Put the work in the vise at 45°

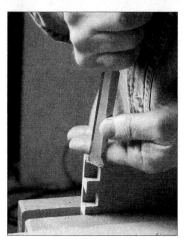

▶ **The finished joint,** ready for trial assembly.

Joining the parts

▼ *Enter the tails.*

▼ *Close the joint with a hammer.*

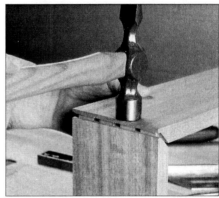

▲ *The lap should sit down tightly.*

▲ *The miter should close snugly.*

Find the tight spot

If the joint won't close because the fit is too tight, you will have to locate and ease the tight areas. How to deal with this and other joint problems is explained in Chapter 4, *Misfits*, page 107.

CHAPTER 7

Making a secret miter dovetail

Regarded as the most difficult joint to make in the dovetail family, the secret miter in fact requires no new sawing or chiseling skills. Prepare two pieces of wood 18 in. × 4½ in. × 11/16 in. Both pieces must be the same thickness. Face sides are inside.

Marking out

You make six lines (three sets of two) using two gauge settings. Position the flat side of the cutting gauge knife away from the fence.

First gauge setting, two lines

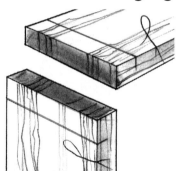

1 & 2   Mark the pin and tail shoulder lines

Set the gauge to the thickness of the wood. From the end grain, mark across the face side of each piece and about one-third of the way across each edge.

◀ *First & second lines – both pieces viewed from face side.*

Second gauge setting, four lines

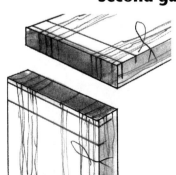

3 & 4   Mark the first rabbet lines

Set the gauge to 1/8 in. From the end grain, mark across the face side of each piece and across the edges to within 1/8 in. of the far side.

◀ *Third & fourth lines – both pieces viewed from face side.*

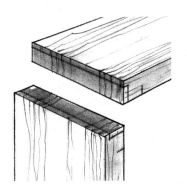

5 & 6 Mark the second rabbet lines

From the face opposite the face side, mark across the end grain and across both edges to meet the first line.

◄ *Fifth & sixth lines* – *pieces in correct postion, face sides inside.*

Two aspects of this gauge line suggest faulty technique. First, it's gauged from the wrong face – the face opposite the face side. However, because you carefully thicknessed the work, gauging this way will not make the joint less accurate. Second, the knife is sited wrong way round in the gauge. However, since the corner of the rebate must meet the miter line and since the corner of the rebate will become a miter, this too will not noticeably affect accuracy. It's simply not worth the effort to change the gauge setting in pursuit of a perfect joint. After gauging the joint lines, miter the edges.

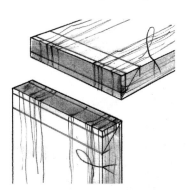

◄ *All gauge lines* marked, plus miter, both pieces flipped.

Cut the two rabbets

Cutting rabbets for a secret miter is the same as for a double lap *(p. 119)*. Use a shoulder plane or a table-mounted router.

◄ **Rabbets** *cut in the pin and tail pieces of a secret miter dovetail.*

Lay out the joint

Making a secret miter differs from the other three dovetail joints in one major respect. Whereas "make tails before pins" is the rule for the through dovetail, single lap, and double lap, with the secret miter you have to make the pins first, then use the pins to mark out the tails. Use the same layout as for the single lap practice joint in *Ch. 6, Mark the tails, p.120.*

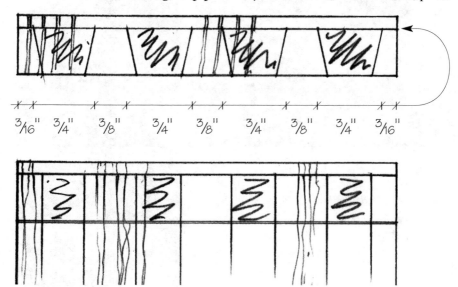

$3/16"$ $3/4"$ $3/8"$ $3/4"$ $3/8"$ $3/4"$ $3/8"$ $3/4"$ $3/16"$

▲ **Determine** *how many glue lines the joint requires as with a double* *lap dovetail. Equal size pins and tails are easier to cut.*

Mark the pins

◀ **Mark out** *the slopes on the end grain with a sliding bevel and square the lines down the tail piece.*

Saw the pins

Before you saw the pins, remove most of the miter waste with a shoulder plane. If you leave this operation until after sawing the pins, the rebate return will be cut-up by a row of small cuts, making planing more difficult.

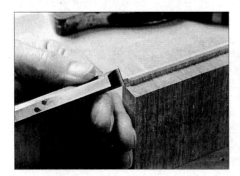

▲ **Cut the miter** *end with a chisel to prevent breakout when planing. Remove most of the miter waste by shoulder plane.*

► *Saw the pins.*

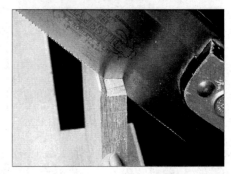

Chisel out the waste

▼ **Chop** out the bulk waste.

▼ **Check** your work.

▲ **Cut the face** of the pins using the sawn surface as a reference.
▶ Cut out the end wall of the tail socket using the rebate as a guide face.

Mark the tails from the pins

You now have to position the pin to mark the tails, an operation best done by clamping the parts in place on the bench. Had you made the tails first and tried to mark pins from tails, you would now realize that it's impossible to access the pin sockets to mark out the joint. Clamp lightly at first and adjust the parts to the correct position by tapping with a hammer. Once positioned, tighten the clamps.

◄ *Position* the pin piece over the tail piece and clamp the setup firmly.

▼ *Mark* the tails. You have to access the tail socket from the face side of the work. The secret miter is the only dovetail joint that requires this procedure.

▲ *Establish the ends* of the tails on the corner of the work, then square across the end grain with a knife line.

▲ It helps if you identify which areas have to be cut before you commit with saw and chisel.

Saw the tails

▲ **Because** you have to saw at an angle down the face of the tail piece and at right angles to the end grain, I frequently change all the rules and saw down the face first.

Chisel the tails

▲ **Cut back** to the shoulder lines, then clean out. You can use a mallet, but tap lightly.

Make the miter

▼ **Put the work** horizontal in the vise and saw to the miter line.

▶ Since this miter goes to a feather edge, use the technique on p. 106 Use a wide chisel, but cut the outer tip last.

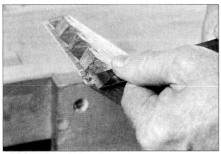

▲ **Complete** the miter at both ends.

▶ **Finish** the miter across the board with a shoulder plane, using the chiseled miter at each end as a guide.

◀ **Close** the joint.

CHAPTER 8

Making other dovetails

To this point I've focused on the dovetail as a corner joint to join relatively wide boards. However, the dovetail has always had a role as a rail joint and is frequently found so used in historic as well as modern hand-made furniture. There are three major types:

- dovetail halving
- dovetail housing
- drawer top rail

As with corner joints, the details of each rail joint may be varied.

Dovetail halving

The dovetail halving is found on large frame structures such as post and beam houses and barns as well as on smaller frames such as weaving looms and farm implements. It's seldom used as a furniture joint because two flat pieces meeting at a T-junction is an unusual furniture configuration.

Begin by marking out the tail piece.

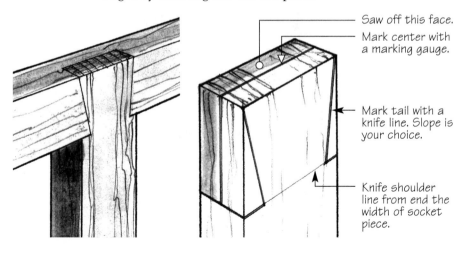

Saw off this face.

Mark center with a marking gauge.

Mark tail with a knife line. Slope is your choice.

Knife shoulder line from end the width of socket piece.

Making the dovetail halving

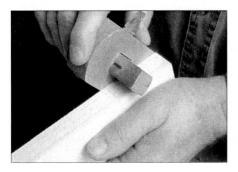

▲ **Set the gauge** *on center and gauge the center line.*

▶ **Mark the slope** *with a marking knife. Darken with a pencil for visibility if needed. The knife line is insurance: it provides a registration mark for cleaning up with a chisel if you fail to cut a straight line with the saw.*

Sawing off the face is like sawing a tenon. Here's the sequence.

◀ **Angle the work** *in the vise. Begin the cut on the far edge and cut a 1/8-in. (3mm) kerf across the end grain. Saw to the waste side of the line.*

◀ **Cut down** *the line nearest you, from back corner to front shoulder line. Keep the teeth fully in the kerf to avoid ragging the kerf on the end grain.*

◀ **Turn the wood** *around in the vise and saw to the near shoulder line.*

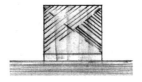

◀ **Mount the work** *vertical in the vise and saw down the remaining triangle of uncut wood to the shoulder line.*

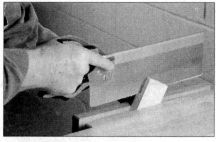

◄ ▲ *Photos show grip and saw position for the sawing sequence illustrations on previous page.*

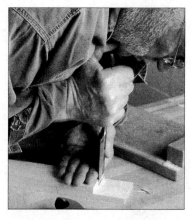

▲ *Remove* the back face.
► *Clean up* the shoulder by vertical paring.

◄ *Saw* carefully down the angled line.
▲ *Clean up* the shoulder.

Fitting the dovetail halving

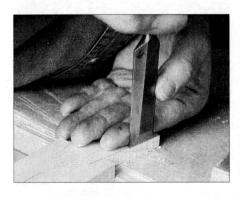

▲ **Here's where** you claim your insurance. If the sawn line needs improvement, register the chisel in the knife line and clean it up.

▲ **Clamp** the workpiece to the bench. Position the tail piece supported by the cut off face and mark the joint as if it were a large through dovetail.

▼ **Mark** half way line with gauge.
▶ **Hold work** on a sawing board and saw to within a small chisel cut of the line.

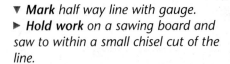

▲ *Mount work* in the vise and clean out the waste. Establish the finish line at each side, leaving a mound in the middle, then flatten the mound. It's a horizontal version of cutting the end grain in a tail or pin socket.

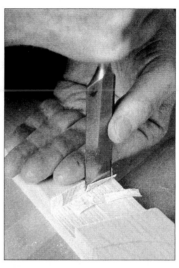

▲ *Clean up* the shoulders by vertical paring.

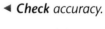

◄ *Check* accuracy.

▲ *Fit the joint.*

▲ *Cut parts* of a dovetail halving.

Dovetail housing

A housing is a groove which runs across the grain. A dovetail housing is frequently found on the front and back stretcher rails of a chest of drawers. Since the rail must be entered from the outer edge, there is no way to hide the dovetail housing other than by covering the edge with a strip or molding.

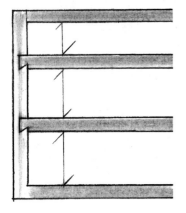

You must cut the housing in exactly the right place. However, precisely centering a dovetail is hard to do. The solution is to make a half dovetail rather than a full one. The rail has a square edge on the top and a dovetail slope on the bottom. The "dead stop" square shoulder ensures that you get the drawer opening the same dimension at each end, with parallel stretcher rails, and accurate dimensions. The single slope provides plenty of holding power.

Prepare a practice rail piece 18 in. × 2¾ × 3/4 in. (450mm × 69mm × 19mm) with square ends. The chest side piece in the accompanying photographs is about 14 in. (350mm) wide.

Set a cutting gauge to 7/16 in. (11.5mm) and gauge the shoulder line on the face side of the rail. Continue the line about 1/4 in. (6mm) on both edges.

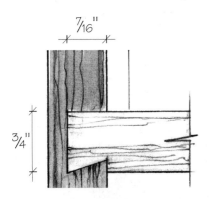

▲ *Make a full size drawing of the edge of the joint as shown above.*

◄ *Jack the work comfortably high in the vise. Mark the slope on both edges with a marking knife. Begin the slope at the corner of the wood.*

◀ ▼ *Cut* the shoulder line, leaving a short 1/16 in. (1.5mm) to chisel. Don't cut beyond the knife line.

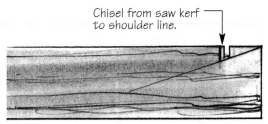

Chisel from saw kerf to shoulder line.

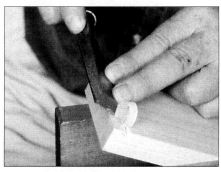

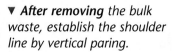

◀ *Fashion* the dovetail slope by horizontal paring with a wide chisel. Work seated with the workpiece mounted in the vise at a comfortable angle. As the cut proceeds, guide the chisel by resting the flat of the back on the newly cut face. Keep off the corner – this is a roughing out rather than a finishing operation.

▼ *After removing* the bulk waste, establish the shoulder line by vertical paring.

▼ *To establish* the exact slope of the tail, put the chisel in the knife line and vertically pare about 1/4 in. (6mm) at each end.

▲ **Return** the work to the vise and clean out the waste using the two edge cuts and the corner as your guide to accuracy.

▲ **Check** the work.

◀ **Square** across the face and the edge of the case side to mark the dead stop shoulder line.

▼ **Mark** the depth of the housing – same gauge setting as for the shoulder.

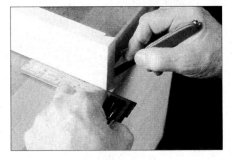

▲ **Set** a marking gauge to the width of the rail, 2¾ in. (69mm), and mark the inside edge of the rail.

▲ **Mount** the case side in the vise so that its edge is level with the bench. Position the rail with a try square and mark the slope with a marking knife, then square the second shoulder line across the housing.

Excavating the dovetail housing

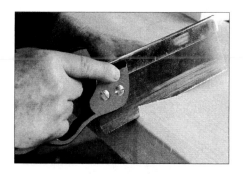

◀ **Saw** to chiseling distance from the knife lines. Like any single lap socket, this cut must start on the corner nearest you. On old furniture you will often find the worker sawed way past the end gauge line to make the chiseling easier – it's not necessary.

◀ **Begin** by chopping a line half way down the length of the housing, then chisel the bulk of the waste, working within the saw kerfs.

▲ **Establish** the shoulder with a wide chisel. Power by muscle or tap with a mallet.

▲ **Check** the accuracy of the angled cut using the sliding bevel against the back of the chisel.

Fitting the dovetail housing

▼ **Clean** up the bottom by horizontal paring.

▶ **Check** bottom with depth gauge.

◀ **Enter** the joint. Ease it if necessary.

▲ **Check** the joint and move on.

◀ **Two rails** fitted in dovetail housings.

Drawer top rail

The drawer top rail joint is basically a single lap joint with a shoulder line variation. It's used on the top front and back rails of a table fitted with a drawer. Success depends upon careful marking out to get the offset shoulder lines in the right place. Make a drawing to determine the dimensions. You can't begin making the joint until the ends of the table have been glued together.

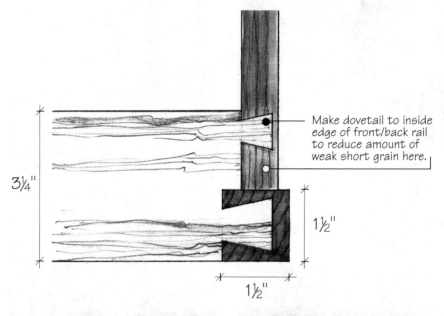

Make dovetail to inside edge of front/back rail to reduce amount of weak short grain here.

$3\frac{1}{4}$"

$1\frac{1}{2}$"

$1\frac{1}{2}$"

▲ **Mark** *the two shoulder settings with a cutting gauge. The distances are worked out by measurement alone: there is no "take off" from the leg-rail assembly.*

▲ **Cut** *the tails and clean up.*

Laying out the drawer rail

▼ *Use a cutting gauge* set to the thickness of the rail to mark the shoulder at the socket depth.

▼ *Set up* the leg assembly in the vise as if you were marking out a single lap joint. Position the tail piece flush with the edge of the leg and square to the assembly.

▼ *Mark out* the sockets as in a through or single lap joint.

▶ *Use a pencil* to square down from the knife lines.

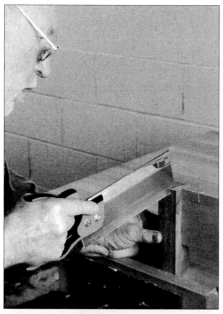

◀ ▲ *Saw* the sockets.

◀ *Chop* out the bulk waste.

Fitting the drawer top rail

◀ ▼ **Clean up** the joint and check for accuracy.

◀ ▲ **Enter** the joint and tap home with a hammer. Plane the rail flush after assembly.

Index

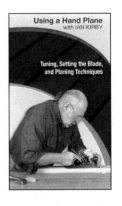

Editor	Larry Grainger
Photography	John Kelsey
Drawings	Ian Kirby
Production Manager	Morgan Kelsey
Page Layout	Larry Grainger